This Is Stevie's Story

DOROTHY GARST MURRAY

This Is Stevie's Story

REVISED AND ENLARGED EDITION

Introduction
by Pearl S. Buck

02217

ABINGDON PRESS
NASHVILLE ♪ NEW YORK

THIS IS STEVIE'S STORY

Copyright © 1956, 1967 by Dorothy G. Murray

Library of Congress Catalog Card Number: 67-11711

SET UP, PRINTED, AND BOUND BY THE
PARTHENON PRESS, AT NASHVILLE,
TENNESSEE, UNITED STATES OF AMERICA

Introduction

THIS BOOK, so tragic in its story, should be introduced upon a note of joy and optimism. For the long silence is broken, the deathly silence of parents and public in regard to their retarded children. All too long indeed has the retarded child been hidden in silence, for until we dared to speak and to listen, his plight has gone unredeemed. He has not been able to speak for himself, this poor child, and in the midst of life, he has lived, as one dead, waiting to be revealed.

Now, thank God, there are those who speak for him; and who can speak more eloquently than his parents? No longer surrounded by false shame, the parents of retarded children are telling their story, revealing their sorrow and their love, demanding for their children the same right that other children have in our free society, the right to opportunity for growth and happiness.

Mrs. Max Murray, of Roanoke, Virginia, is one of these parents. She shares with us in this book her son Stevie. Let us read it with reverent and tender attention. It is the story of one and of millions.

—Pearl S. Buck

Foreword

THIS STORY about one boy and one family reveals much about the forces that shape our society. Compassion and determination, vision and practicality—these in mixture brought a better life for Stevie. They are bringing a better life for millions who share his limitations but who have the same rights for dignity and happiness.

The short span of his life marks a revolution in attitudes toward the mentally retarded and services for their betterment. Milestone after milestone has been passed. Classes, clinics, workshops, camps, and activity centers now exist where none, or very few, existed a few years ago.

The prospect is now that within Stevie's lifetime there will be a full array of services in every community for mentally retarded children and adults. For babies yet unborn, there is the hope that research will unlock further the secrets of prevention and that mental retardation will join other ills of man that were scourges of the past.

Yet the confrontations ahead will be many if we are to achieve that ultimate goal.

Diagnostic and health services still are not accessible to all. The adolescent and the adult are often slighted. Persons in rural areas frequently are missed, though traveling clinics are feasible. There is a great need for case finding and early treatment for the mildly retarded.

In *residential care* there is only just emerging the variety of community facilities that will bring living for the retarded to new plateaus of dignity and convenience.

In *education* qualified services must replace instruction by unqualified teachers, in unsatisfactory classrooms, with unsuitable teaching materials.

To prepare retarded persons for *employment,* school and work must be related and realism achieved in providing the opportunity for lives of maximum independence.

The range of needed *protective services* must be expanded to include modernized civil and criminal law, guardianship, insurance, social security, and guidance.

In *research and prevention* twin goals must be insisted upon—(1) the support of basic research that will unlock the secrets of reproduction and development; and (2) the application of that knowledge in programs giving improved quality of services and measures of prevention.

To achieve these larger expectations will require more than the struggles of parents, more than the perseverance of teachers, physicians, and counselors. It will require the generative force that can come only from interested citizen support—from you the readers of *This Is Stevie's Story.*

New York City
August 22, 1966

Luther W. Stringham
Executive Director
National Association
for Retarded Children

Preface

THE MANUSCRIPT for *This Is Stevie's Story* was written in 1954, when services for the mentally retarded at a community level were almost totally nonexistent. In 1956 private publication of the original edition was underwritten by interested individuals who believed the book would provide concrete guidance and encouragement for the thousands of parents of the mentally retarded who were struggling to make a place in the world for their children. Over the past ten years I have received letters and personal expressions of appreciation from hundreds of parents of the retarded as well as from many professional persons working in their behalf. The wide acceptance of the original publication and the continued demand for it have resulted in the present edition.

This volume contains the two parts of the original edition just as it was published in 1956 plus an Epilogue which brings the story up to the present time. The fact that the Epilogue could be written in 1966 with a much more hopeful outlook is due in no small part to the quiet social revolu-

tion which has taken place during the past ten years in behalf of the mentally retarded everywhere—a revolution
brought about by the National Association for Retarded
Children and those agencies, both public and private, which
are helping to establish a network of comprehensive services
for the retarded throughout the country. In grateful recognition of the fact that our Stevie's story could never have
ended so happily had it not been for the activity of the
NARC during the past ten years, my husband and I are
assigning all royalties from the present edition to NARC
for further promotion of its work in behalf of the mentally
retarded everywhere.

The decision to share our mentally retarded son with the
public by telling his story was not an easy one. It came after
years of suffering and the consequent desire to do something
constructive for other parents of such children. The basic
reason for the writing of the book was a twofold one: first,
to bring a measure of comfort and courage to the thousands
of parents who face the unsolvable problems involved in giving birth to a retarded child; second, to bring the wide scope
of the problem of mental retardation to the attention of the
general public. It has been my sincere conviction all along
that the dearth of facilities for the proper diagnosis, care,
and training of the retarded has been because of a lack of
knowledge about the total problem on the part of the general
public rather than because of cold indifference. The vast and
sweeping changes for the better which have taken place since
the increase in public understanding have justified this belief.

We tell the story of our own son with the hope that it

will further serve to point out to our fellow citizens the pathetic plight of the mentally retarded and their need for human compassion and understanding as well as for more adequate services appropriate to their needs. The story is told, too, in the hope that it may help those parents who are struggling with this heartbreaking problem more nearly to understand themselves as well as their children. Finally, the story is told in the sincere belief that it may bring some bit of additional light to this long misunderstood and neglected sociological problem which has faced mankind for so many centuries. It is toward these ends that we are sharing our Stevie and his story.

—Dorothy Garst Murray

Acknowledgments

No BOOK is ever the product of one mind alone. As the author of *This Is Stevie's Story* I am indebted to many persons. First, to my wonderfully wise parents, the numerous teachers, friends, and others who had a share in molding and shaping my life so that the telling of this story was possible. Second, I owe a debt of gratitude to those parents of retarded children, writers, and professional persons who read the original manuscript and offered much helpful and constructive criticism. These included Pearl S. Buck, Stanley High, Edith Stern, Dale Evans Rogers, Gilbert Hanke, Salvatore G. DiMichael, Joseph E. Barrett, M.D., Willard D. Boaz, M.D., Marrianne Kornfeld, Psychologist; Judge Odessa P. Bailey, the Rev. J. J. Scherer, the Rev. Merlin E. Garber, Jesse H. Ziegler, the Rev. Robert E. Richards, Earl H. Kurtz, Ora W. Garber, Jerome Natt, M.D., Mrs. Helen Smith Mugler, Miss Louise Davis, Mrs. John Norman Harvey, Mrs. Jack Laskin, Mrs. Caressa Morgan, Mrs. Ruth Cuddington, and Luther W. Stringham, who offered much constructive help on the Epilogue. Special appreciation is extended to Pearl S. Buck, who read the manuscript initially and later consented to write the introduction to the book, and to Mrs. Christine Arrington, who typed the manuscript. Last, but deepest of all, is my gratitude to my husband and our children for so generously sharing their wife and mother that the world might be made a bit better for Stevie and all such children who will follow. They have given up more than anyone will ever know in making my work for retarded children possible, and they have done so with a generosity of spirit which has given me the courage to keep going in the face of many difficulties.

Shortly after completing my manuscript I discovered these words by James Francis Cooke which express more accurately than any words of my own how I feel about what has been written in this book:

> The moment of triumph is always very dangerous.
> Because you believe that you have made
> Your book,
> Your picture,
> Your drama,
> Your symphony,
> Your victory.
> Poor fool! Poor fool!
> Do you not realize that you are merely
> The glove on the hand of God?

If in a small way this book will serve to bring some measure of encouragement and faith to other parents and to provide enlightenment to the general public on the problems posed for society by mental retardation, then I shall consider it my rare privilege to have served as a mere "glove on the hand of God."

—*Dorothy Garst Murray*

Roanoke, Virginia
1966

PART I

Chapter One

Two o'clock in the morning is a wonderful time for thinking—and for dreaming great dreams if one can become sufficiently awake to do so. It was mid-April, 1945. A great wave of hope was passing over the world that a cessation of armed hostilities would soon take place in Europe. The very air was electric with the excitement of momentous events about to take place. As I sat nursing my baby son, who was only eight weeks and a few days from heaven, I was indulging in some of those dreams that mothers have dreamed from time immemorial as they cradled helpless infants in their arms. If there is any satisfaction in the world that can compare with that which comes from taking a hungry baby from bed, ministering to his physical needs, giving him food, and then holding him over one's shoulder for a bit of cuddling, as yet I have not found it. It was in this satisfying mood that I was doing some thinking that April morning.

Looking about the dimly lit room, I could see all the physical necessities brought together for the needs of one small baby, among them the quaint bed lovingly created by my father for his own children. The little bed, made from a cherry tree on our farm, had provided the first resting-place for all the members of my own family and for my first two children. I thought of the anxious days and nights my mother and father must have spent by this bed during the illness and death of their firstborn and the serious illness of another child—days when miracle drugs were unheard of and the only things to which parents could turn were their own good common sense and a not-too-well-trained country doctor.

My father seemed very close that morning as I held in my arms this baby who had been named for him. Father had died only a few days after my eighteenth birthday, and it had always been a sorrow to me that he did not live to know my husband and children, as well as his many other grand-children. He loved children with all the fullness of his great heart and was never happier than when holding several on his knees.

I thought of the weary months and years of war through which the world had just passed and was almost thankful that he had not lived to see the terrible devastation which had taken place, the inhumanity of man to man, but most of all the suffering which had been imposed on helpless women and children. I thought of the mothers throughout the world who at one time had held their babies and dreamed dreams for them, babies who had grown to manhood and were now dead or dying on battlefields.

As I sat holding my son over my shoulder and rubbing my cheek against his fuzzy little head, I breathed some prayers along with my dreaming: prayers that I might have the wisdom so to train and teach him that he might grow up to make a real contribution to the good of humanity rather than becoming cannon fodder for those who had been so misled and misguided as to believe that the problems of the world could ever be settled by hate and war; prayers that perhaps this child might follow in the footsteps of his grandfather, who had been a minister and a great power for good to every life he touched.

As one thought led to another that April night, quite suddenly I had a very strong feeling—call it premonition or what you like—that for some reason or another this child was to be very close to me, would need me very much, perhaps a great deal more than either of my other two children would. At the time I simply attributed this feeling to the fact that he bore my father's name. Perhaps if I were wise enough, it might be my privilege to help him develop into a great spiritual leader. I remember this night as vividly as if it were only yesterday and recall telling myself that no matter what kind of tie there might be between my life and his, it must never seem apparent to the other children that he was favored or that my concern for him was any greater than for them. Cruel scars can develop because one child is seemingly more important in the eyes of the parents than other brothers and sisters. My mind was made up that, if it were

humanly possible to achieve, not one of my children would
have cause to feel that another child in the family received
preferential treatment.

After much back-patting the inevitable burp finally came,
and I tucked the now-sleeping baby back into the little bed,
adjusted the covers, and went back to bed for a few hours'
sleep before beginning a new day at six o'clock.

The musings of that early morning hour were completely
forgotten in the rush of the busy days that followed. Being
the mother of three children leaves little time for musing or
reflecting on past musings; consequently it was not until
almost four years later that the memory of that night, a
memory which was then so painful that it seemed to sear
my very soul, came back to me with sudden clarity. It came
back on the day I was to discover that the tie which would
bind this child to me was not one which would result in
glorious achievement for the benefit of mankind, but a tie
so grievous, so heartrending, so permanent that only death
itself would ever break it for either of us; a tie which filled
me with such mental anguish that for weeks I lived in a
world filled with pain and hopeless despair and the terrible
knowledge that I was the mother of a mentally retarded
child. For on a bleak, gloomy day in January, 1949, we came
face to face with the knowledge that this beautiful, solemn-
faced little boy, whom we had all learned to love so much,
would never grow up, that no matter how perfectly his body
developed it would always be possessed by the mind of a
child. This was to be the tie which would bind me to our son

—the baby son for whom I had dreamed those dreams that warm spring night of long ago.

Chapter Two

WE THINK now that the first two years following Stevie's birth were the happiest years of our lives. War came to an end in Europe not many months after he was born, and shortly afterward our war with Japan ended. People began to have hope once again that perhaps mankind could at last live together in peace. Our business was doing well, and life was filled to overflowing with the mere joy of living. Our oldest child, Anne, was in her first year of school and was bringing home daily the priceless bits of information that only a first-grader—and particularly the *first* first-grader— can bring! The second child, Andy (Max Andrew for his daddy), was going through that delightful period of imaginary playmates. With Anne away at school most of the day and Stevie too small to play with, he was not the least

bit discouraged by the lack of playmates; he simply created
some in his own imagination. His favorite was "Banal
Hoober," and the hours they spent together provided entertainment for Andy and many priceless memories for me. We
always told him that Banal Hoober was the nicest playmate
he ever had, because he never left his cap and galoshes to be
returned to a harassed mother at a later date; he never
tracked mud on my kitchen floor; he was always quiet and
polite; and we didn't even miss the cookies he took when he
and Andy raided the cookie jar together!

Stevie was as near to being an angel as a baby could have
been. He rarely ever cried, except when uncomfortable, and
his physical development was perfect. Although he was
somewhat later than the first children in walking and feed-
ing himself, we were not alarmed, as he was a large baby
for his age, and we did not encourage his walking until he
seemed ready for it. We know now that there were symptoms
of mental retardation from a very early stage. Because we did
not know what they meant, we just assumed them to be personality differences and gave no thought at all to many
signs which we would now view with definite concern in
a small infant.

At two Stevie was far behind most children of that age
in his mental development. All attempts at training proce-
dures were met with seeming indifference, and he made no
effort to talk or to imitate the behavior of others. We were
not unduly alarmed, however, because we realized that children develop differently, and we were still sure that with
time and patience his training could be accomplished. We

felt, too, that when verbal communication became important
to him, he would make some effort to talk. Along about
this time he began to exhibit certain mannerisms and obsessions that we did not understand, but this was a case,
I suppose, that "where ignorance is bliss 'tis folly to be wise."

On the first day of November, 1947, our baby girl was
born, and it was without a doubt the happiest day of our
lives. Conditions had arisen about three weeks before her
birth which made both my husband and me realize that her
delivery would not likely be a normal one, and there was
even the possibility that it could be fatal to the baby. After
three weeks of anxious waiting, she arrived quite suddenly
in the pink of condition. Although it was a breach birth,
there were no complications, and since I had had only a
small amount of gas, I had the rare and delightful privilege
of announcing to my husband that we had another baby girl.
After the birth of each of our other children I had been so
sleepy from medication that he had to tell me the good news.
This time I told him. When the nurse brought her to my
room and we had our first half-hour together with this new
baby, our joy knew no bounds. At last we had our perfect
family: two boys, two girls.

The days that followed were such busy ones and so filled
with happiness that the lack of Steve's development simply
did not register as it should have—at least not as much as it
would have had he been an only child or had I had more time
to be conscious of his difference from the other children of
his age. Although he began to cry a great deal more than
when he was a tiny baby and still made no effort to talk, we

just told ourselves that when he was ready he would talk.

In the summer of 1948 we took all four children on our usual camping trip. Max and I had enjoyed camping so much before the children were born that when they came along, we decided to start them out early. Now I must confess that it isn't the easiest thing in the world to go into the woods and set up housekeeping for a week or more with several children, particularly if there happens to be one in the diaper-and-bottle stage. We had done so, first with one child, then two, then three. Now we felt perfectly competent to manage with four.

Since Elaine was only nine months old, we decided it would be wise to stay reasonably near home in case of an emergency; so we chose a lovely state park within seventy miles of our home. It was the only camping trip in all the years of our married life that was a complete and hopeless failure from almost every standpoint. Since that week was the beginning of a gnawing and growing fear concerning Stevie's mental growth, I feel that some account of it must be included here to give a true picture.

Before the first night was over, I had begun to wonder about the wisdom of our adventure. The camping area was especially crowded that weekend; and we had very little real privacy. Although our nearest neighbors were very nice people, they were the kind who wanted to sit and talk and be very friendly every hour of the day and evening. One of the reasons we like to go camping is to be alone with our family and away from too many people. We like to be friendly with our fellow campers to the extent of sharing food now

and then, or perhaps sitting about a campfire in the evening
to sing songs and share experiences; but for a large part of
our time we like to be left to ourselves to read, play games
with the children, or just rest. There were four adults in our
neighbor's party and one cute, irresistible little boy just
Stevie's age. Actually it was the first time in Stevie's life that
we had had an opportunity to observe him for any length of
time with a child his own age. The difference in their abilities
was so marked that even the older children seemed aware
of it.

The strangeness of our surroundings, the lack of his usual
sleeping arrangements, the effect of constantly being stared
at by our neighbor campers (who, we knew within a few
days, were making some very pointed observations about our
queer little boy)—all tended to make Stevie more agitated
and irritable than he had ever been in his life. So it was with
reluctance and yet a sense of satisfaction that we finally decided to cut our trip short and go home several days earlier
than we had planned. Before we were to go, however, I
was to recognize that perhaps Stevie's condition was more
serious than we realized and could not be regarded lightly in
the belief that he would outgrow it.

Our camp neighbors had a man and his wife come in one
evening to spend the night and the following day with them.
The woman was one of these openly inquisitive people, with
no feeling or respect for the privacy of anyone about any
matter. You are likely to meet them anytime, anywhere, but
those met while on vacation seem to have an insatiable desire
to gather information about their fellow vacationers. She

questioned me repeatedly as to what Stevie could or could not do. It was not the thoughtful, kindly questioning of a person really interested in the welfare of the child. She spoke in the manner of one of those morbid people who attend funerals simply to stand and gaze at the grieved ones to see "how they take it." After realizing that our conversation was rapidly approaching the point where I might be tempted to be rude, I asked to be excused, on the pretext that I needed to see about the children.

At the time I resented what I felt was intrusion into our personal affairs, but we now know that perhaps it was much easier for strangers to bring us to an awareness of our little son's limitations than it would have been for a member of our family or a close friend. Her parting thrust was one with which parents of retarded children have been cut to the heart down through the ages: "Well, if he were my child. . . ." I did not stay to hear what she would do if he were her child. I only wanted to shout at the top of my voice: "Yes, if he were your child, you would do just precisely what I am doing: the best you know how to do from one moment to the next." Good taste forbade such a reply; so I went back to my tent darkly reflecting that it was a pity someone had not developed a repellent which would be as effective in keeping inquisitive acquaintances at their distance as was the handy little gadget with which we sprayed our tent to keep away the flies, gnats, and mosquitoes.

I did not tell my husband of our conversation. I felt it was needless to worry him with the opinions of an idle, talkative woman, but as I lay in our tent that night after he and the children were asleep, an icy fear began to grip my heart that perhaps something really *was* wrong. For hours I tossed, and that night was only the beginning of many sleepless nights for several years to come. Finally in the wee small hours I dropped into a troubled sleep, but not without first deciding that immediately after reaching home we would make an appointment with our pediatrician for a thorough checkup for Stevie. I realized that if trouble were ahead we would gain nothing by postponement. We must face it.

Chapter Three

"Is HE sleeping well?"

It was our pediatrician speaking. After returning from our camping trip we made immediate arrangements to take Stevie to him for a physical examination. After checking him thoroughly, the doctor as he sat at his desk asked many pertinent questions while Stevie was in the examination room being dressed by the nurse.

"Well, no, as a matter of fact he isn't and hasn't been

for some time, but we have just felt it was a passing phase that would soon disappear," I answered.

"What about the baby—how does he react to her?"

"To tell the truth, he just doesn't react at all as far as we can see. He doesn't pay any attention to her. She could very easily have been a new piece of furniture moved into the house for all the attention he has given her."

"What about the other children—does he play well with them or seem interested in the things they do?" he asked.

"Not very much. Most of the time he appears to exist in a little dream world of his own, and the rest of us just don't seem to enter into the picture, not even his daddy and I."

My reaction was one of surprise that the doctor asked this particular question. We had more or less assumed that it was just Stevie's disposition to be utterly indifferent to those about him, and the fact that it could have any particular bearing on his other characteristics made me realize that this entire situation had many facets that had never occurred to us.

There were other questions, many of them: What about his toilet training? Did new places and people seem to upset him? How much did he talk? What about temper tantrums? Did he seem to understand the commands we gave him? How did he play with his toys? These and many more the doctor asked as he sat thoughtfully, with long intervals between each one. To each, I had to answer that his reactions were far different from those of our other children at his age.

"Well, I can't find anything wrong physically. His adenoids and tonsils are a bit large, but they aren't diseased. I wouldn't advise having them out until he is a little older, as they could easily grow back at this age, and it would be necessary to do it all over again." That was a long speech for Dr. Roberts, for he was a man of few words.

As Stevie came out of the examination room, it was apparent that the physician was observing him quite closely. He darted about the office giving first one thing and then another his attention, but only for a fleeting interval.

Finally after a few more questions Dr. Roberts picked up from his desk the card containing Stevie's medical record and his notes, glanced over it casually, and said: "There doesn't seem to be anything we can do right now; he may snap out of it; children often do, and when they begin to develop socially it happens suddenly. I would suggest that we just go along for another few months, and, if he doesn't seem to be showing some development by Christmas, perhaps we had better have Dr. Jones look him over."

Dr. Jones was a brain specialist, one of the few psychiatrists in our city. That in itself should have caused me more concern than it did. I knew that children as well as adults frequently had certain emotional difficulties, and that it was becoming more and more a practice to refer them to a psychiatrist if the medical doctors could find no physical reasons for certain symptoms; however, this suggestion gave me little cause for real alarm.

I asked a few more questions about dealing with specific situations. Dr. Roberts assured me that I seemed to be doing very well and that I could continue the same course I had been following in most respects.

"Try to see that he gets plenty of rest and bring him back in December for another visit."

I left his office that day feeling somewhat reassured by the fact that there were no serious physical symptoms apparent. Now, as I look back, I feel rather certain that our pediatrician had a definite concern about some things that we ourselves had considered quite unimportant.

As summer waned into fall, the day-by-day struggle of trying to care for the children as I should was becoming more and more a burden to me. Andy started to school, so there were only two children at home during the school hours. But Stevie became a bigger problem than ever. During the daytime he was like a flitting, restless little bird. Darting here, there, everywhere—upstairs, downstairs to the basement for a few minutes, outdoors to play in the sand for five or ten minutes, then back into the house to start the same routine over again. His toys held little or no interest for him for any length of time.

The one source of entertainment which never palled, however, was poking objects into our warm-air-furnace registers. His toys, combs, brushes, silverware, jewelry, money, anything he could find that was not fastened to something, went down the register. Sometimes it was a bit amusing, but when precious minutes had to be spent trying to retrieve lost articles, such as a quickly needed pair of scissors, it soon ceased to be funny. Max became quite adept at retrieving things with a bent wire, but some things, such as silverware and combs, had to be rescued after another fashion; and the amount of time we spent hunting for things that had disappeared and then getting them out of the particular register into which they had been thrown, began to be extremely important. Finally, in sheer desperation, we covered every register with a piece of coarse screen wire with holes about one-fourth inch in diameter. That only added interest to the game, for now Stevie had the challenge of finding something small enough to go through the screen! Pins, needles, bobby pins, screws, small bits of paper, wire, or string—it was really wonderful how many things could be pushed through a quarter-inch hole if one took the time and had the patience to do it! If he could find a screwdriver, the screws would come out. Off would come the screen, then the screws, screen, screwdriver and all would go down the pipe with several magazines, toys, combs, and doll babies for good measure.

The nights weren't much better than the days. After a few hours' sleep he would often wake up to spend two, three, or four hours rocking back and forth on his hands and knees, or humming tuneless little songs to himself, or sometimes hysterically laughing or crying. By now we were really alarmed because all our efforts to comfort or reassure him seemed to fail utterly. Neither my husband nor I was physically or mentally fit to meet the demands of our daily living after spending three or four such nights every week.

When, after our apple harvest was completed in November, one of my sisters and a friend offered to keep the children for a few days so that we might have a complete change of routine, we did not hesitate for a moment in accepting their offer.

We had four wonderful days, from Thursday until Monday, in Washington and New York. It was the carefree, happy weekend of two persons very much in love with each other and with life; a joyous, bright, and lilting prelude to the somber movements which were to take place in our life's symphony within the very near future.

Chapter Four

By ALL rights, Christmas that year should have been wonderful, but it wasn't. Anne was ten, Andy six, Stevie not quite four, and Elaine a bright-eyed, eager fourteen months. We were all in excellent physical health, and we had every reason to have a happy holiday. I had always loved Christmas—everything about it: the joyous, eager, and secret gift preparations; the fruitcake and cookie baking; the house and tree decorations; good wishes from friends coming in daily by way of the mail; the school and church programs with their cherubic angels bringing the story that was so old yet ever new. Then the final hush of Christmas Eve, after the children were all sleeping peacefully, as Max and I tiptoed about putting the final gifts under the tree: the tricycle too big to be wrapped; the doll sitting primly beneath the tree branches waiting to come to life in the arms of a loving little mother; all the other gifts of love that go into the making of a happy time being brought together for that long-awaited Christmas morning when the children would come tripping to our door, hours before dawn, to call out excitedly, "It's Christmas!" One event of that Christmas stands out in my mind so clearly that I now believe it was possibly the first genuine feeling of fear that all might not be right with our little son's mind.

After hearing Daddy read the Christmas story from Luke and having family prayer as had been the custom in both my family and Max's, and now in our own, the big children delved eagerly into their packages. Even the baby's eyes were filled with starry wonderment as she sat in her high chair and tore the paper from her packages, having almost as much fun with the paper and ribbon as she did with her presents. The paper was perfect for rattling, and each piece must be tasted so that something good to eat would not escape her notice. She soon discovered, however, that the primary purpose of the paper was to hide the gift, and that what was on the inside was what really mattered.

Stevie did not seem very excited over his presents, which had been bought with much care and hope that here at last would be something he could really enjoy. He gave them a quick look, glanced over the room littered with paper, string, and presents, saw the happy faces of the other children, then dashed upstairs to get on Andy's bed and rock back and forth on his hands and knees. How many hours of his life were spent at this pastime would be hard to estimate, but he seemed to find some consolation in the rhythm of swaying back and forth. I sat there by the fire that morning with my heart feeling like a stone. There was no escaping from the reality that such a reaction to Christmas by a little boy who was more than "half-past-three" was not a normal one. The fact that we had an appointment to see Dr. Jones on January 10 at the recommendation of Dr. Roberts, our pediatrician, who had seen Stevie again shortly before Christmas, added to my feeling of uneasiness.

January 10 was a beautiful, sunny, winter day. By the time breakfast was over, lunches packed, the children off to school, the baby to grandmother's, and the house in a reasonable state of order, I was somewhat exhausted. When I reached the doctor's office for a 10:30 appointment, I was more tired than afraid. Both my husband and I had enough work to do that we did not spent much time in needless worry.

Dr. Jones was an acquaintance of ours in an indirect way. During the days when he was in medical school his youngest brother and I had been good friends, and I remembered the pride with which Robert had always referred to his oldest brother who was studying psychiatry. He was also a member of the religious denomination to which Max and I belonged, and we occasionally saw him at various meetings. He came to our own church once in a while, as his sister-in-law was a member of our congregation. So it was not as a total stranger that I entered his office that morning with Stevie.

He immediately put me at ease by inquiring about my mother and several of our mutual acquaintances and also by giving me some news of Robert and his wife and children. He took Stevie on his knee and tested his reflexes with his little rubber hammer. We both had a laugh when Stevie promptly took the instrument from his hand and pounded a bit on the doctor's knee. He asked numerous questions, many of the same ones Dr. Roberts had asked, but also many, many others. All the time I was answering questions, he was taking notes, thus giving me the opportunity to point out some of our greatest difficulties in knowing how to deal wisely with our little boy. After a while he casually suggested that it might be wise to have some X rays made and asked what I thought about it. I assured him that we wanted to do what was best for the child and would do anything he advised. He promptly made arrangements to have it done that same day as there was an X-ray technician in the same building. I listened as he made arrangements over the telephone, calling attention to certain areas of the brain in which he was particularly interested.

He also suggested, even more casually, that there was a boarding school only five miles from our home which was owned and operated by a teacher trained in work with children whose mental development had not been normal. He wondered if I might like to talk with this teacher, whose name was Mrs. James.

"Now the fact that I am suggesting you go there doesn't

necessarily mean I think your little boy is like the children she has. Some few of her children are rather pathetic in appearance, and you may feel unduly alarmed at seeing them. Most of my work has been with adults, and I do not feel qualified to express an opinion about your child just yet." He paused for a moment, then added: "My lack of experience in this field makes me feel it would be wise for Stevie to be seen by a person who has spent years in the study of such children."

"Do you think this teacher will talk with me?" I asked.

"Yes, I believe so, but I will telephone her if you like."

I asked him to do so and he assured me he would call that day for an appointment.

After receiving her name and telephone number from him, I left the office with Stevie, who by this time was becoming quite bored and restless with the entire procedure.

We met my sister, Miriam, who had gone into town with me to do some shopping. The appointment for X rays was at two o'clock, so by the time we had eaten lunch it was time for this ordeal. I say *ordeal* because taking Stevie to the doctor for anything had always been such. He not only wanted to turn all the lights on and off, but the doctor's instruments fascinated him, and I always expected to have to pay for a valuable piece of equipment in addition to the professional fee. The X-ray laboratory was just too much. Everywhere there were switches to be pushed or pulled, lights of different colors to turn off and on. It was only by sheer force, and some ingenuity, that the technician managed to get X rays and take Stevie out before he wrecked the place.

I went home so utterly tired and depressed that the events of the day seemed like a dull nightmare. My first reaction was that I would delay seeing the teacher a day or two, but then, on second thought, I decided to go the very next day if an appointment could be made.

As I left Miriam's home that afternoon, she said: "I'm glad you're going to see Mrs. James tomorrow; after all, if there *is* anything wrong, we won't gain anything by waiting." When I looked at her, the expression on her face made me believe that she was much more gravely concerned than my husband and I were and had possibly been so for some time. Many months later I was to find that I had surmised the truth.

I went home to make the appointment with Mrs. James and to prepare and serve the evening meal. After tucking the children in for the night and relating to Max the many experiences of the day, I fell wearily asleep, hoping that perhaps the X rays would reveal some pressure on the brain, or some abnormal physical condition relating to the brain, or just anything that might possibly be corrected by an operation.

My hope that the X rays might provide an answer to the cause, and thereby a hope for cure, were in vain. A telephone call to Dr. Jones the following morning brought the news that the X rays did not indicate any source of trouble. There were no signs of pressure on the brain at any point, or any indication of damage or injury to the brain either in the past or at present so far as the X rays revealed.

All hope was now lost that some physical cause could be

responsible for Stevie's strange behavior. We were now
face to face with the fact that our child's problem was not
so simple as we had innocently believed for several years.

Chapter Five

THE AFTERNOON for our visit to Mrs. James was
bleak, cold, and gray. Although there was not an actual down-
pour of rain, heavy moisture in the air caused droplets of
water to fall from the trees and bushes. It seemed as though
the very world of nature wept in sorrow that day for the
news that I was to hear about our little son. We approached
the school grounds somewhat apprehensively shortly after
noon. The school was located in what was once a lovely old
colonial home. I remember thinking it was most unusual that
such an institution was in existence only five miles from our
home, and we had never heard of it. I had been told that the
house originally had belonged to one of Grandmother

Murray's cousins, but we had been unaware that it was now a private boarding home for exceptional children.

We were met at the door by a maid who ushered us into the combination office and living room. It had a delightfully warm, cozy setting with every indication of gracious living. As I waited for the matron to enter, I wondered what type person she would be. My eyes roved over her pictures, the draperies, the grand piano in the corner, and her choice of magazines and books, and I felt immediately that here lived a person with whom I had much in common.

I could hear Mrs. James across the hall directing her "children" into their various occupations—the small ones being sent to bed for a rest period and the older ones to the playroom. Several of them, realizing there was a stranger in the house, came to the door of the room in which I was seated to peek in with childlike curiosity. There were two or three Mongoloid children, and even to my untrained eye it was visible that they were mentally afflicted. Immediately I had a deep feeling of compassion for them. But when one cute little fellow came, I could not help but notice the beauty of his face and the fact that he looked just like any other child. "That's strange," I thought almost aloud. "I wonder what in the world he's doing here." The fact that a child could look just like any other child and not be normal mentally was one which had never occurred to me at any time. That was the beginning of the discovery of a great many facts which had never occurred to me simply because it was a problem which had been kept completely hidden from the eyes of the world.

After the children were all settled at their various after-lunch occupations, Mrs. James came in to talk with me. I introduced myself and thanked her for allowing me to come, because I knew by now that she must be a very busy person with the energies of all these little people to direct. I noticed that she, like the doctors, had been observing Stevie closely. In a short time he wandered over into the playroom across the hall with the other children, and she assured me that I need not worry about his damaging anything. She was a person with whom one could feel immediately at ease, and I soon found myself talking freely with her about Stevie. She so completely understood the problems with which I had been coping for so many months that it was an immeasurable relief just to pour out my troubles to her. She asked questions, many of the same ones the physicians had asked, and I answered them as honestly as I knew how. After we had talked at some length she said: "Well, Mrs. Murray, it looks very much to me as if your little boy might be mentally retarded." In all my life, even with the copious amount of reading I had done, I had never seen the term in print, nor could I recollect ever having heard it. I knew quite well what *mental* meant and also what *retarded* meant in its usual sense, but the two words used together just didn't make sense to me.

"What do you mean?" I faltered. "Do you mean there is something wrong with his *mind?*"

"Yes. Many of the symptoms are present, and even though one cannot say definitely in one so young, there is a grave possibility that it is true," she answered quietly.

We sat there for a few moments as the realization of what

she had said gradually penetrated my numbed brain. The room and all the world swam dizzily around me, and it seemed that suddenly I had been catapulted into another sphere only to be returned in a matter of moments to the one I was in as an utterly new and different person. By this time my eyes and voice were choked with tears, but within seconds I had gained sufficient control of myself to begin asking questions. They had been asking me questions, I thought ironically; now I would ask some.

"But how in the world can you tell? He looks so normal . . . his physical development has been perfect . . . and he was such a good little baby." The words came tumbling from me. I pointed out all the things he could do, the many, many things which were so obviously all right with him, as though I were trying to convince her as well as myself that this terrible supposition about Stevie could not be true.

She pointed out many things to me, quietly, patiently, as though I were a small child trying to absorb some very stubborn facts for the first time. She explained that there were many such children who looked just like all other children, some of them unusually beautiful children, in fact.

"But what causes it? So far as I know there is nothing like this in either my family or my husband's," I said. I had vague recollections of having heard at one time or another that certain types of mental abnormalities ran in families.

"Yes, you are thinking in the mistaken terms in which people have thought for generations, simply because they don't know. These children can appear in *any* family, regardless of whether there has been one before."

She went on to explain that although there could be some types of mental deficiency passed from one generation to another, in addition there were other causes, including injuries to the brain tissue at birth, disease, or accidents, and probably many unknown causes.

"Is it a temporary condition, one which he may outgrow?" I asked hopefully.

"That is impossible to say. If it is real mental deficiency, then there is no known cure or treatment. Neither is there hope that he will outgrow it. However, in some small children there can be apparent retardation which may be caused by an emotional factor. In such cases there is the possibility that with proper care and specialized treatment these children may stand some chance of reaching so-called normal or average intelligence," she replied.

We talked on and on. I asked her if there were any way possible to tell just how much development there might be, or what the future might hold for him. She pointed out that although there were certain tests and ways in which it was possible to ascertain some facts about the situation, it was virtually impossible to make definite predictions, especially in one so young. She explained some of the advantages of early training by a person with special education in this field. When I asked her if she would consider taking him as a day pupil, she assured me that this would not work out in her particular school, because of several factors which were quite reasonable and easy for me to understand.

Realizing that the time had gone by rapidly and feeling sure that she needed to be about her work, I arose to go.

We walked to the playroom to get Stevie and found him apparently quite at home with the little children who for one cause or another would always be just that—little children.

I thanked Mrs. James for the time she had given me, for her compassionate understanding, and for the information she had furnished from her many years of experience in working with retarded children. As Stevie and I walked hand in hand out the door into the cold, bleak January afternoon, the contrast between the room we left behind seemed symbolic. I knew instinctively that we were now moving from a warm, secure, happy world, in which we had lived with a good daddy and three other children, into a new one: a world which had been created by misunderstanding, by fear, by prejudice, by superstition; a world which would send a greater chill to our hearts than the cold, penetrating damp day could possibly send to our physical selves.

I drove home in a daze, but there were three things that penetrated to my grief-stricken brain: the soft, beautiful music of "The Rosary" coming over the car radio; a cardinal flying across the road in front of me with the brilliant color of his coat a gay contrast to the gray sky and the gaunt, bare trees and bushes along the way; and the sudden overwhelming wish that I could have an automobile accident on the way home that would take Stevie and me both into eternity. That statement will be shocking to many people, and particularly to those who have never faced a severe emotional crisis. But I am sure that many people who read this book can remember times when the overwhelming desire to take the easy way out was overcome only by the inherent instinct of self-preservation.

"Oh memories that bless—and burn! Oh barren gain—and bitter loss! I kiss each bead, and strive at last to learn to kiss the cross." The words of "The Rosary" struck me with a new and terrible meaning. The memory of that April night in which I had dreamed great dreams for this little son came back with sudden and awful clarity; the service of dedication in our church when he was only a few months old, the solemn, sacred prayers offered in his behalf by our pastor in our home in the presence of my husband and the older children and myself; these were the memories that came to "bless and burn" and to shake my faith in the goodness and mercy of God to its very roots—a faith which, though shaken, was never lost.

On my way home I stopped at Miriam's house to pick up the baby. Miriam was married to my husband's brother, and they lived only a few hundred yards from us. She met me at the door and I think must have known by my face the news I had to convey. As was typical of her, she said little and only took me in her arms until my husband came in from the shop where he had been working. With the understanding that comes only from a great heart, my sister walked into her bedroom and stayed there until after I had told Max. His first reaction was not one of grief but just incredulous disbelief. I am sure that had he been with me during the interrogations of the doctor and Mrs. James and heard all the things they said, it would have been much easier for him to believe that it *could* be true. As I had been, until after my interview with them, he had absolutely no knowledge of anything concerning mental deficiency. Neither of us had seen more than a dozen or so mental defectives in our entire lives, and the amount of knowledge which we *didn't* have was astounding.

We took the baby and Stevie and returned to our home. I went to our bedroom and there gave vent to all the pent-up emotions and fears which had been tormenting me for months. The torrent of tears brought a certain amount of relief, and into this release came the words of a poem by Grace Noll Crowell which I had memorized several years before my father's death. It had been the only prayer I could pray for weeks in the necessary readjustment after losing a beloved daddy. Once again it came back to provide me words with which to petition for courage to go on.

> God make me brave for Life,
> Oh, braver than this!
> Let me straighten after pain
> As a tree straightens after rain,
> Shining and lovely again.
>
> God make me brave for Life,
> Much braver than this!
> As the brown grass lifts let me rise
> From sorrow with quiet eyes
> Knowing Thy way is wise.
>
> God make me brave—Life brings
> Such blinding things.

Help me to keep my sight,
Help me to see aright.
That out of the dark, comes Light.

The children rushing in from school brought me to the realization with which women have been confronted since the beginning of time—that no matter what happens, no matter how little reason there seems to be to go on living, where there are children one must at least go through the motions of living as long as the heart beats and there is strength to walk.

Max stayed with me instead of going back to work, and we went through the evening household routine together. Just having him in the house brought comfort and reassurance. After the evening meal was over, the four children bathed, "storied," and tucked in for the night, we were once again alone with our thoughts. We decided that if Dr. Jones could possibly see us again the next day, we should perhaps seek his advice about many questions that were already beginning to come into our minds as to what would be our best course to follow. Although neither Dr. Jones nor Mrs. James felt that it was possible to give a complete and final diagnosis just at this point, we were at least aware that Stevie's mental condition was such that we could no longer continue in the naïve and hopeful belief that he would outgrow it.

Chapter Six

Max and I had both come from a religious background. For four generations our forebears had lived in the simple traditions of our faith. Perhaps it was because of this background that through all this experience we never for one moment doubted the existence of God or his goodness and mercy to us as his children. There are people who, when face to face with an emotional crisis, sometimes doubt the very reality of a heavenly Being, or if they do believe, it is with the conception of a tyrannical One who causes people to suffer just because he has the power to do so.

Through all the long, dreadful hours of that January night, there were two thoughts that constantly returned to my mind; two thoughts that rose like spirits from the dead to haunt me, because they were memories of conversations which had taken place in my life many years before, and both of those with whom I had talked were dead.

It was a warm summer night in the depression summer of 1934. Daddy and I were lying on our backs in our yard looking up at the star-spangled sky. We were talking about a news item which had been in the paper that particular evening. A brilliant, wealthy, and socially prominent student had committed suicide on the previous night at our state university.

"Why, Daddy, why in the world would anybody who has intelligence and social position and no worries about money or a job for the future take his own life?" I asked. In my naïve seventeen-year-old mind I had somehow arrived at the conclusion that if one had education, position, and no worries about money, he had everything needed to make life worth living.

"It's a lack of God in people's lives, honey; without him life has no meaning, no purpose, and people become so confused in their thinking that they see no point or reason for going on in a hopeless situation," he answered quietly. We talked of many other things that night, but before we went to bed he made this statement which so firmly fixed itself in my mind that to this day I can hear his voice as though it were only yesterday: "Never leave God out of your thinking, and no matter what comes, what crisis you may face, your thoughts won't confuse or baffle you."

It was as simple as that. He hadn't said: "Now when you face a crisis, *if* you can find God. . . ." He hadn't said there would be an answer to every question, that we would know the reason for everything; only that if God were included in our thinking and reasoning, our thoughts would not lead us to a dead end. Perhaps it was the memory of those words which made it possible for me to face his death with serenity less than two months later. Daddy's advice led my thinking to the complete assurance that even death itself was a part of God's plan and that in the final analysis the all-inclusive plan must be a *good* one, simply because it was his.

This is not to say that in the initial stages of our grief for Stevie we were either wholly submissive or ready to accept the fact that we were the parents of a retarded child.

As all such parents know, this realization takes weeks, months, and in some cases even years to accomplish. But it does mean that throughout that period of our own lives, because God was included in our thinking, it became possible for us to say: "How can God use me in this crisis? How can this mental and spiritual torture mold me into a person who can be more useful to him?

Am I big enough for this sorrow to make me better instead of bitter?"

This trend of thinking not only made it possible for us to keep going at the beginning, but it put meaning into our plans for the future. All this seems very simple and easy to accomplish stated in so many words, but the struggle to abide by this philosophy instead of crying out, *"Why—why did this have to happen to me?"* was a never-ending one. We clung to it weakly, hopelessly, at first, because it seemed all we had to cling to; but as years passed and the wound began to heal we believed more firmly than ever that the only way ever to meet a crisis or even to make important decisions was with God in our thinking.

The other conversation which came back to me on that black night had taken place the night of our wedding. Because of the long distance from my home to the church in which we were to be married, some friends of ours who lived just across the street from the church invited me, as well as my bridesmaids, to come to their home to dress. They were one of those beloved couples with countless "love grandchildren" who were not related to them at all but who, nevertheless, considered them as "grandparents." I happened

to be one of these lucky "grandchildren." Granddaddy
Hoover's excuse for inviting us to dress at his home was
that it would save our dresses from becoming wrinkled
from the long ride to the church, but there was a sly twinkle
in his eyes, and I think that no small part of his reason was
that he just loved a wedding and wanted to have a part in
the last-minute flurry of excitement.

We were all dressed and waiting during those last few
breathless minutes before Granddaddy would proudly offer
me his arm to take me across the street. He had loved my
father devotedly, and as he gave me some last-minute fatherly
advice he said: "Ah, it does my old heart good, Dotty, to
see you and Max make this marriage. You're joining two of
the finest and sturdiest family lines I know of, and good
blood will tell, child—it always tells." He went on to say that
from such a home as ours only the finest children would
come.

I suppose it was a foolish thing to remember, an ironic
thing to recollect, but it came to me over and over again that
night: "good blood will tell, child—it always tells." He, like all
his generation and even my own, had no idea that there
could be any cause for defective mentality other than in-
heritance. Because he had known both our families for several
generations, he had great hopes for the children we would
have. I could only breathe a prayer of thankfulness that
Granddaddy had died in his naïve belief that it would be
virtually impossible for anything not good to come from
such a union. We were to find later after much study that

ours was still "good blood" and was not necessarily responsible for Stevie's condition.

The morning after I talked with Mrs. James found Max and me sitting in the office of Dr. Jones for an early appointment that he had graciously given us before his regular office hours.

"I suppose you know why we're here, what Mrs. James told me yesterday," I began.

"Well, not exactly. I thought it was something rather alarming or you wouldn't have wanted to see me again so soon," he said.

Max told him of my visit.

Dr. Jones told us that even though what she feared could not be considered an absolute certainty, there were many things pointing in this direction, and that her judgment was surely to be respected because of her more than thirty years' experience in studying and teaching retarded children. We asked him for his opinion about placing Stevie in such a school as Mrs. James operated. She had pointed out the advantages of early training in the hands of experienced teachers.

"Well, how do you feel about it?" he queried, turning toward me.

"We just don't know. My first feeling is that to uproot him from his familiar surroundings and take him away from home would do more harm than good, but we want to do what is best for him regardless of our own feeling in the matter," I replied.

He went on to say that it was his judgment that if I felt physically able to care for Stevie and the other children we should keep him with us, at least for the time being, perhaps keeping in our minds the possibility of a special training program later. Just before we left his office that day Dr. Jones gave us some advice which I now believe to be the most important and the soundest advice that can be given to the parents of a retarded child.

Here in essence is what he said:

"Max, your greatest problem the next few years is going to be one of not yielding to the temptation to take Stevie here, there, and everywhere for treatments, for tests, for expensive experiments in trying to find something to help him. You can go from one clinic to another, from one doctor to another, having the determination in your mind that *everything* possible must be done for his sake. In my opinion if you follow such a course, at the end your child will be much worse off, you and Mrs. Murray will be more confused, more dissatisfied, more in a state of uncertainty and disbelief than you are right now. You can easily spend ten or fifteen thousand dollars which you may need desperately in later years for Stevie's permanent care. I cannot, at this point, make any definite predictions as to what the future may hold for him; after a few years of watchful waiting we may be able to tell more. This is a field in which little research has been done, and it is a matter in which we must take time and make unhurried decisions."

He did not speak in the dictatorial manner of one who would direct that you follow his course *or else*. He spoke as a friend and as one whose judgment we could respect. We knew that he knew a great deal more about the dangers which were ahead of us than we could know ourselves. He assured us that if there were another doctor we wanted to consult, he would be happy to work with him in any way he could for our benefit. We told him of Dr. Black, a local physician whom we knew quite well; in fact, he was the husband of Max's first cousin. Although at present he was doing general practice, he had a degree in psychiatry and had spent five years working in the psychology department of our State Training School for Mental Defectives in Lynchburg. He had also done psychiatric work during the last war with the Navy. Dr. Jones felt that by all means we should arrange for Dr. Black to see Stevie, not only because of his years of experience in working with such children, but also because he was our general family physician and personal friend as well. He had never had occasion to see Stevie, because we had continued taking our children to the pediatrician who had cared for them since babyhood.

The next morning we were in Dr. Black's office at an early hour, Stevie with us. He did not seem at all surprised to see us as we walked in his office. He inquired after our parents and the other children, and then said: "Well, what brings you in this morning, Max? Is there something wrong with this young lady?" He nodded toward me as he asked it half jokingly, half seriously.

Max smiled somewhat wanly. "No, I'm afraid not; that is, I mean we almost wish it could be something wrong with one of us. It isn't quite so simple as that."

He then told him of our talk with Dr. Jones the day before and also of my consultations with Mrs. James and Dr. Jones.

He began asking questions all over again. He observed Stevie closely the entire time we were there. Finally after about half an hour he stood up, indicating that our interview must come to an end, because his office waiting room was filled with people to be treated for the usual January epidemic of sore throats, infected ears, etc.

"Max, I'm afraid Dr. Jones is probably right. I saw hundreds of these little children in my work at Lynchburg, and Stevie is a mental defective if I have ever seen one."

He spoke with compassion, and yet with the authority of one who knows, insofar as it was humanly possible to know, of the problem which was facing us. At the time these words seemed frank to the point of being almost brutal, but in the months and years ahead we were to look back on that morning with humble thankfulness that here was one who had the moral stamina to bring us face to face with the truth in all its stark reality, the courage to make a deep, clean cut.

"I think Dr. Jones has given you some excellent advice. I would go along with every bit of it, especially the advice not to go all over the country seeking a cure for Stevie. As for the special schools, I have visited many of them, and they are just not for people in average circumstances. Most of these schools charge more to keep a child for one year than you would spend on your entire family. My advice is to forget it entirely, not only because there is some question as to how much he would really benefit by it at this particular age, but also because it might deprive your other children of things they actually need now and, possibly, an education for them in the future. They are building a new training school at our State Home, and if the time ever comes when Stevie needs special training, placing him there, in my judgment, would be far wiser than placing him in any private school you may find," he said.

"Is there anything I can get to read that may help me in knowing how to care for him and train him in some way?" I asked.

"To my knowledge there is not. It is a problem about which little has been said or written. They are doing some research now, and it may be that in years to come there will be answers to some of these questions which confront you, but just at the present there is nowhere I can tell you to turn for help," he replied.* "There are some new drugs being tried for mental defectives right now, and if you like we can put Stevie on those just as an experiment. I can assure you that they will harm him in no way, and they may help his nervous agitation some, but do not anticipate that they will in any way cure his condition."

He reached for his pad, wrote out a prescription, and handed it to Max.

"I'd like to see Stevie again in about a month or six

* The reader will recall that this interview took place in 1949 prior to the organization of the National Association for Retarded Children. Today, a great deal of help is available for parents including printed material as well as services at a community level. For information write: National Association for Retarded Children, 420 Lexington Avenue, New York, New York, 10017.

weeks for a thorough physical checkup. I will be glad to see
him any time before that, if you want to come in, and, in the
meantime, keep in touch with me," he concluded.

We went home, home to begin the weeks, months, and
years of watchful waiting—hoping against hope that there
might yet be a mistake, that Stevie might suddenly "snap
out of it" and in a few months' time catch up with all his
eager little contemporaries who were rushing pell-mell and
full force from babyhood into the delightful state of being
"big children."

Chapter Seven

SOME PEOPLE are born with the compelling force to
act in any given situation, to *do* something; sometimes it
makes little difference whether what they are doing is right
or wrong, wise or unwise, they must be *doing something*
about it. I believe it is this force which sends
many parents anywhere, everywhere, seeking a cure for their

retarded child when there is no cure. This was my own nature, somewhat quick, impulsive, believing something must be done about any situation with which I happened to be connected. These months of waiting, of inaction, of coping with what seemed to be a problem without solution were very difficult for me. Had it not been for the steadying influence of Max's personality, which in this particular respect was different from my own, we would possibly have erred from the advice of both doctors to take it easy far more than we did.

There was one more source of advice we did seek, however. Max had a first cousin who was studying at the Mayo Clinic. Realizing this was one of the finest medical centers in our country, we wrote to him asking him what facilities were available there for the testing and study of retarded children. He had worked with psychiatric cases in the Navy and also had had three years' experience in a mental hospital; so we felt that he surely knew something of the problem we were facing. We knew that mental defectiveness or retardation was not to be confused with mental illness, but since many of the problems faced by the family are similar, we felt he would be in a position to offer us some constructive help. His reply to our letter contained, I believe, some of the soundest, safest, and wisest counsel we received. With his permission, the letter is printed here, word for word, just as he wrote it. It must be remembered that these words of advice came not only from the head but from the heart as well, for Max and he had been close companions from babyhood. They had played, worked, gone to school together, and shared all the joyous memories of growing up together. Ed had been in our wedding, and his twin sister had been responsible for our first interest in each other; so it would have been impossible for these words to come from anyone who was closer to us or more concerned for our happiness as well as for Stevie's.

Dear Max and Dottie,

We fully appreciate the emotions that seethe within you at this time and the difficult decisions that confront you. We want you to know that we share your feelings and would gladly do anything in our power to be of comfort or help to you.

You say that I would be surprised to know that you feel no shame. To the contrary I should be greatly surprised if you did. You are surely too intelligent and too mature for that. Why should you feel shame for a biological accident? And your other clearly superior children are all the proof needed that it is a biological accident. Would you feel shame if one of your children were accidentally struck by a car and his intelligence lowered? Of course not, only sorrow.

When I was in med school, we used to go to a new Presbyterian church. The young minister and his wife were one of the most brilliant and handsome couples we ever knew, Phi Beta Kappa and all that. Their first child was a very low defective. It can and does happen to anyone.

Mental retardation poses a great social problem—one that has never been adequately solved. It is a field all in itself and frankly I am not qualified to advise you except perhaps in a general way. My experience has been with adult psychotics, and in the Navy I had quite a bit of experience with adult defectives. Of one thing I am sure, they must never be allowed to compete directly with normals in anything, for that is a source of continual frustration to them. I have seen defectives develop severe psychoses because of continual frustration occasioned by a constant effort to cope with problems that were to them unsolvable. I have seen them quickly settle down into useful, happy people in the protected environment of an institution where competition was virtually eliminated and their decisions were made for them.

Since you have asked my advice I am sure that you wish me to speak frankly, and I would like to point out a few general principles that from my experience I am sure are sound.

(1) You must accept early in your attack upon the problem the fact that you yourselves will never be able to make objective decisions regarding Stevie. Even I am too close emotionally to be objective, and so I would urge you to take no steps until you are psychologically prepared to accept without qualification expert objective advice. There is no immediate emergency, and I would wait until I was sure I possessed the inner fortitude and determination to follow any course prescribed by an expert. After I was sure of myself I would take Stevie to one of the best child psychologists that I could find and I would follow his advice to the letter, not trusting myself to deviate. As far as I know, Johns Hopkins is one of the best. The University of Virginia has made progress, but it is a relatively new field there. Unfortunately that particular field is not too strong here at this particular time. We have a world renowned child psychiatrist, but his life's emphasis has been on behavior problems rather than mental retardation.

The child psychologist will want to do several tests, and he will be able to then predict with some accuracy at what age level Stevie will be able to perform, and that will determine in great measure his advice to you.

(2) The second general principle is one which may look obvious, but I have seen it ignored so often that I feel I must mention it. Do not neglect your other superior children for the sake of Stevie. It is a parental instinct to protect the weak, and the weaker the child, the more powerfully does this instinct manifest itself. I have seen—not once but scores of times—parents pour out all their money, love and attention upon a defective or psychotic child and leave their normal children starved for affection and deprived of the advantages that should have been theirs. That is comparable to a man spending all his money and labor on a rocky hillside that can never be made to produce, and at the same time letting his fertile fields grow into thorns and briars. Such a course can only compound one's disappointment and sorrow.

(3) The third principle is a corollary to the second. One must guard against unconsciously pushing his other children to outstanding performance to compensate for the poor performance of the retarded one. I have seen that happen with most unhappy consequence.

(4) Finally, in this life, one must learn to cooperate with the inevitable. The mark of a great person, of a truly wise person, of a Christian, it to be able to accept the inevitable. There are those who hide their eyes in the sand, those who struggle to change that which cannot be changed, and those who figuratively hurl defiance at God and man. But those who accept that which is ordained for them are able to cooperate in God's plan as it affects them.

Situations such as these throw our helplessness and finiteness into such bold relief. Kay and I would be so happy to give all that we have if we could but be of some concrete help to you. This poor letter seems such a weak offering.

In closing, we want to encourage you to count your many other blessings and to strengthen your courage and faith.

Much love,
Ed

Today, the worn and dilapidated condition of his original letter stands as mute testimony to the many times it was read and reread during those early days. I had an opportunity later to share it with another mother whose own retarded son was only one day younger than Stevie. She, too, felt that the counsel it contained was well worth sharing with other parents.

The first and foremost problem which faced us now was the decision as to how and what we should and could tell our family, and neighbors about Stevie's condition. There were two courses open to us: We could keep the information we had gained the past few days completely to ourselves and act as though the situation simply did not exist, or we could tell exactly what the situation was. We chose the latter course. (We now feel, without a doubt, that this absolute frankness is the most painful and yet the most healing balm that can be poured into the wounded hearts of parents of retarded children.) My husband and I had both been active throughout our married life in church and civic affairs; although we were not socially or politically prominent, we had a very wide circle of friends and acquaintances, as well as broad family connections. We felt that trying to hide or ignore Stevie's condition would not only be harmful to our own sense of right and wrong but would, worst of all, be an extreme injustice to the child. Stevie needed understanding from our relatives, friends, and neighbors, not sometime in the distant future but *now*. Feeling emotionally incapable of doing the telling ourselves, we asked my sister to tell our friends and close neighbors exactly what we had found out. She wrote each member of our families. The only person I myself told was Mary Byrd, one of the women who lived on our farm. Mary had helped me one afternoon each week since Stevie was a very small baby. Next to the members of our families, it was she upon whom I leaned more heavily for the next few years than any other person. She had the rare gift of complete understanding of such little children, and Stevie loved her devotedly. Mary was one of the very few people he ever called by name; having heard me address her as Mrs. Byrd, he chose to call her Birdie.

I believe that to those who knew us best our attitude of frankness and openness was not surprising, but to many persons it seemed to be absolutely unthinkable. This is a good place to point out a reaction on our own part that was surprising, even to ourselves. From the very first day we realized that our little son would probably be a mental cripple, we had absolutely no feeling of shame or disgrace. Many people acted as though we should not only hide the child but ourselves as well. To be very honest, we were a bit surprised that we did *not* feel any shame; but there was none—only a terrible and overwhelming grief that this little child whom we loved so dearly would possibly grow up with a bewildered and confused mind, simply because he did not have the capacity for coping with the problems of ordinary existence.

We soon discovered that it was almost impossible to treat a mental problem in the family with the same objectivity as a physical illness, because people just can't think in those terms. Since the beginning of the human race, any type of mental abnormalcy has been regarded with fear, superstition, and misunderstanding by the general populace, and no matter how much one may want to look at it openly and objectively, it is a most difficult thing to do. This false feeling of shame or disgrace which results from having hidden mental problems from the world for so long has a far more serious psychological effect on the families involved than the actual mental problem itself. Many persons develop a bitterness and resentment against all humanity from which they never seem to recover. At this point in our experience, both my husband and I resolved that if any opportunity ever came our way, we would surely help to lift the veil of misinformation and sheer superstition which had surrounded mental illness and mental defectiveness. That this opportunity would come far more quickly than we ever expected, we did not know.

Perhaps a conversation with our pastor and his wife helped to set our path in that general direction. On a warm, sunny afternoon less than a week after we had first discovered the tragedy which faced us, I stopped at the parsonage to talk with them. It is hard to say for whom I had the most sympathy that afternoon, for them or myself! I had done much pastoral calling with my father, and I knew his heaviness of heart when he must help lead some of his parishioners through a severe emotional crisis. Since our minister was younger than my husband, and his wife several years younger than I,

I almost felt I should be bringing them comfort that afternoon, rather than seeking help for my own heavy heart.

They already knew about Stevie because we had asked my
sister to tell them. We talked of many things, of our interviews with the doctors, how we might best deal with certain
situations that would arise, and how this might in a very
definite way limit our time for contributing to the program
of the church. I told both of them that we felt the greatest
need they could help meet right now was to tell our friends
and the church members the truth about the entire situation.
Max was the superintendent of our Sunday school and as such
was known by many persons who did not know either of us
intimately. We knew there would be much speculation, much
talk, much rumor about "something being wrong with the
little Murray boy's mind." We asked our minister to tell
exactly what we ourselves knew to anyone who asked him
and even to broach the subject himself in any situation where
he thought it wise to do so. It has always been a firm conviction of mine that nothing in the world is so effective in
putting a stop to mistaken rumors or speculation as the truth
about a situation, and we felt that surely no one was in a
better position to present the truth without any embellish-
ments than our friend and pastor.

In his knowledge of the reaction of human nature to sudden
tragedy, he supposed, I am sure, that it was quite within the
realm of possibility that we were struggling with a guilt com-
plex in addition to our grief. Sensing this, he told of the instance in which a blind man was brought before the Master
by some of his acquaintances, and they in their legalistic and

sardonic way of thinking, inquired: "Master, who did sin, this man, or his parents, that he was born blind?" And Jesus answered, "Neither hath this man sinned, nor his parents: but that the works of God should be made manifest in him."

Pastor Harley pointed out that even though the plans of God are often beyond our human understanding, in every situation similar to this the possibility existed for its being used that the glory of God might be made manifest.

I had been very close to my father during the last four years of his life, possibly the most formative years of my own. He did not enjoy driving a car; so for those four years a very great portion of my time had been spent driving him from place to place. A large share of the studying of my high school days was done with my books propped against the steering wheel of our Model A Ford while Daddy did pastoral calling, or sitting on the back pew of a church while he met with other clergymen for board meetings. This close association with Daddy helped me to develop a more mature pattern of thinking than most teen-agers had. It also caused me to absorb many of his fundamental philosophies for living. Among these was the belief that sorrow, constructively used, could be the means of bringing out the very best that any person had to give to the world. I had often heard him say: "Sorrow can make you better, or it can make you bitter; grief carries within itself the possibility either to make you or to break you; it is altogether up to the individual."

Those years with my father had given me an insight and understanding that made it possible for me to believe with our minister that perhaps even this tragedy which we faced could carry within itself the possibility for good, for some worthwhile service to humanity. To this one thought we clung, with the tenacity of a drowning man, during the bleak days that followed.

Chapter Eight

LESS THAN two weeks after our discovery of Stevie's mental limitation, I was made aware of a bit of philosophy so valuable to the parents of retarded children that it surely should have a place here. For several years I had been at the head of a woman's organization involving about twenty-five local groups and covering a rather wide territory. Our annual meeting, which involved a lengthy business session, lunch, and two inspirational talks, had been scheduled for January 23, only thirteen days after I had talked with Mrs. James. All arrangements had been completed months in advance, but there were always last-minute details to be arranged.

My first thought was that I simply could not stand in front of all those women, many of whom had known me since childhood, and preside over a business meeting while my heart felt it would literally burst with grief. Had I lost a member of my family by death, or had one of the family been physically ill, it would have been quite simple to explain my absence. But in no way I could imagine would it be possible to make an excuse for my absence without giving rise to much unnecessary speculation. I decided it would probably be easier to go ahead and preside at the meeting than to answer all the questions if I did not. I was to discover that morning that a strength far over and above our own is available and that in this strength unbelievable things can be accomplished. It didn't help much to know that the members of my cabinet and a few close friends were sitting out in that vast sea of faces wondering if I would be able to go through the day without breaking. It was during the worship service that the bit of philosophy to which I referred above was stated.

The speaker had only recently come face to face with a grief of her own—her only daughter, a lovely and talented girl, had developed a serious condition for which at that time there was no known treatment or cure. It was from the depths of her own burdened heart that she urged us to live day by day, to live in "day-tight" compartments, not trying to delve into the future but just taking one day at a time and knowing that we would always have strength to get through "just one more day." I truly believe that of all people in the world, no one can need this day-by-day philosophy of living so much as the parents of retarded children. At times the burden becomes so heavy, the future so uncertain, the body so numb and weary with the struggle merely to meet the physical and emotional needs of such a child, that many parents come to the place where they believe they just cannot go on; and we couldn't if it were not for that inner source of power which such parents have to develop or completely break with the struggle. It is a way of life that can come only with practice and perseverance, but I believe it is a philosophy toward which we should all strive, regardless of whether we ever completely achieve our goal.

This day-by-day idea does two things: It helps us do a better job during the day in which we are working, and it saves much strength and energy when we deliberately refuse to worry about how we will face future problems. Worry is one of the most exhausting forms of thinking one can indulge in. Every mother of a retarded child can remember the long, sleepless night hours of worry which rendered her completely unfit to meet the needs of her family the following day. It is difficult, but not impossible, to learn not to waste energy in useless worry. This does not mean that our concern is any less, but it is surely a worthwhile discipline of our minds to work toward that goal in which we can live day by day and let faith come in and help dispel the waste of energy created by worrying over things that probably will not happen anyway.

In the days, weeks, and months that followed, Max and

I alternated between high hope and utter despair. Like all parents of retarded children, we saw and magnified the many things Stevie *could* do, while perhaps closing our minds (consciously or unconsciously) to the things he could *not*. It is a never-ending enigma not only to parents, but to professional persons as well, that the mentally retarded will sometimes be very apt in one particular area of behavior, yet in all others be far, far below average. We are told that some few of these children are even on the border of genius in certain fields, yet they are inherently defective. For this reason, it takes many of us entirely too long to believe that our own child is mentally retarded.

For several months after we realized what Stevie's condition probably was, we thought there was very definite improvement in his ability to do things and comprehend what we said to him. Because of this we held on to the hope for many, many months that perhaps there had been a mistaken diagnosis, that possibly by some miracle Stevie would suddenly "come out of it" and develop rapidly to make up for lost time. We believe now that his apparent improvement came about simply because of our wiser understanding of the situation. Before, we had been expecting behavior of him somewhat commensurate with his age, an expectation which was utterly beyond his ability to fulfill. When we adjusted our expectations of him to the level normal to a child of about one year instead of four years, he in turn became happy and relaxed and was able to accomplish many things that heretofore had seemed impossible. All of us tried to give him more personal attention, to help him gain security in what to him must have been a very bewildering world. It was as though he had suddenly walked from the unhappy world of shadow and darkness into the bright sunshine of understanding and love.

At this point we needed to make many patient explanations to our older children that even though Stevie seemed to demand more of our time and concern, our love for all of them was as great as it could be. We explained to them that even though Stevie was four years old, his little mind had not grown along with his body, and we must realize that he could not do many of the things that Elaine could in spite of the fact that she was two years and eight months younger than he.

It did not take us long to discover that in spite of wanting to treat this situation in the perfectly open and frank manner we would have done had it been a physical illness, it just couldn't be done. Not only did the majority of our friends feel that they should not ask about Stevie, but in many cases I sensed their genuine embarrassment if I so much as mentioned his name. Today I hold as priceless the memory of those few people who from the very first shared our deep concern and were big enough, wise enough, and understanding enough to ask about him and give me the opportunity to pour out my terrible grief to them. Pages could be written on this one thing—the psychological impact on the parents of having a grief which they cannot unburden because of the pressure of public opinion—but it is sufficient to say that this aspect can cause more real suffering and wreak more real havoc to the personalities involved than the mental retardation itself.

And it is with a genuine spirit of deep thankfulness that we remember that those who loved us best did not try to hold out a false sense of hope that all would be well. Many people in their effort to be helpful will repeat stories of "So-and-So," who was just like this child and who today stands as a crowning achievement of intellect. Yes, we heard many of those stories from well-meaning friends, but to this day I've never been able to find proof of one.

Many parents will be quick to say: "But I didn't want to talk with anyone; I didn't even want the public to know!" Would such parents feel the same about losing a child by death? Of course not. If a child developed a serious physical ailment, and there was doubt about his recovery, would the parents not believe it very strange if the neighbors, relatives, and friends did not call to ask about him, to express concern for his welfare, and to make an effort to let them know they shared this dark hour of pain? Indeed we would. And yet, in the face of a tragedy which is more grievous than death, more awful than any physical ailment that can strike, we cannot have the solace and comfort of our friends for fear they will embarrass themselves and us as well.

Our physicians had cautioned us over and over from the beginning to try, insofar as possible, not to become so aware of Stevie's difference and so concerned about it that our tension would be passed on to him. They pointed out the very obvious danger of making such an issue of it that he himself would begin to absorb some of our emotional upheaval. For my husband, this was not too difficult because he was away from the house most of the day and must necessarily have his mind centered on the work in which he was engaged. For me, this was an almost impossible assignment and one in which I often found myself failing dismally. When an opportunity developed in the late summer of 1949 which challenged me to get my mind off Stevie and onto something else, and was also an experiment of supreme worth, we decided to plunge in.

It was a hot, stifling morning in mid-August. The older children and I had been gathering together our camp gear and packing for another camping trip. Suddenly I remembered there were a number of unopened letters on the desk and decided that perhaps I should run hurriedly through them to see if there were any that demanded attention before we went away. One of the letters was from our church headquarters asking us to help find homes, preferably rural ones, for one hundred German high school students who were to be brought to the United States for a year's stay under the sponsorship of the German Cultural Affairs Committee, our own government, and our church, the Church of the Brethren. Our small denomination is known as one of the historic peace churches, having as one of the strong tenets of its faith the belief that war is un-Christlike and that the evils of the world must be cured by love and goodwill rather than by hate and aggression. We had been doing relief work throughout Europe all during World War II. At the ending of hostilities it was decided that as a first step toward international understanding this student exchange program should be carried out, and the German Cultural Affairs Committee approached our relief workers about the possibility of locating some of the students in our church homes.

Many times during the days of the war I had felt utterly ashamed that we had suffered so little when many people were suffering so much. We had the comfort and security of our own home, plenty to eat, clothes to wear, and all the necessities of life taken for granted, and above all our home had remained intact. Max's two unmarried brothers were in service, and he was deferred, not only because of the children and myself, but also because of the urgent necessity for agricultural products. When this letter came, presenting an opportunity to do something really constructive toward helping right the terrible chaos of the world as well as to make amends to one who no doubt had suffered everything during the war years that we had not, it seemed almost as if God himself were tapping me on the shoulder and saying: "Now, look, here's your chance to do something about this situation; we'll see if you're big enough to do it!"

I took the letter and rushed over to where Max was working.

"How would you like to have a new member in our family right soon?" I asked. "Here, listen to this." I read the letter to him. We talked for almost an hour. We thought of the opportunity it would provide for our children and us to learn at firsthand of the life and culture of another country; we talked of the potential there was in such a program for creating understanding between the peoples of the earth; we spoke of the tremendous responsibility of taking a seventeen-year-old girl into our home to be a member of our family when the pattern of her thinking would of sheer necessity be extremely different from our own. There were many possibilities and many problems, but over and above it all was the ringing challenge that it seemed a good thing to do.

"There's something else that I think might be of real value in our particular situation," I said.

"What's that?" Max asked.

"Well, you remember how the doctors have emphasized the fact that we shouldn't let our concern for Stevie become so great that it would transmit itself to him; now if we get one of these students, at least I will have to get my mind off him for a while, because I'm sure there'll be too many problems involved in this adjustment to leave me any excess time to worry over him," I answered.

Three hours later found us in the office of our county school superintendent to get a signed statement from him to the effect that such a student would be accepted in our local high school. He was most enthusiastic about the program and urged us to take one if we felt we possibly could.

Thus it was that within less than eight weeks, Gretel came to be a member of our family for one year. Although her name was Gretel, she asked us to call her Margarete, which was the American equivalent, and considering the fact that we could never say "Gretel" with the same soft, beautiful intonations she used and was accustomed to, I can't say I blamed her for wanting the Americans to call her by another name! Margarete's moods were like the sky during an April shower, bright, warm, and eager one hour; the next, dark, cold, and forbidding. The story of her year with

us would fill a book itself—and this is Stevie's story. But
her year with us in relation to him was an important one,
because it gave me one year in which I was forced to use my
mind for more constructive purposes than brooding over
his condition.

Margarete was blessed with one of the most original and
gifted minds it has ever been my privilege to know. She had a
discernment of human nature that few people acquire in a
lifetime. As I now look at that year in retrospect, I think
I learned far more from her than she could have learned
from me. She was a direct descendant of one of Germany's
most famous military leaders of World War I and had been
reared in the typical Nazi tradition of holding little respect
for weakness or frailty of any kind.

I cannot say for a certainty just what Margarete's first
reactions were toward Stevie; there were many times when
I thought I sensed a feeling of contempt. We explained to her
shortly after her arrival that Stevie needed special understanding because his mind could not comprehend things like
other children of his age. For a while there were times when
we knew that he was most irritating to her, but as the
weeks turned into months, her love and compassion for him
grew. Before she left us her joy in his every little accomplishment was as great as our own; and there was a special soft-
ness in her voice when she spoke of Stevie that was never
there for anyone else in all America. Stevie loved good music,
and so did Margarete; this one great pleasure they could share
in common, and as they often sat listening to records or the
radio I could not help but wonder what thoughts went through

the minds of this little boy, who, though at home, wasn't able to enter fully into the joy of that home, and of this tall, stately, blue-eyed German girl who was so far from her beloved homeland. Margarete taught him some simple little folk dance steps, and I can picture them yet, dancing about our living room, Stevie's face radiant in the fact that here in this one thing he could participate *with* someone; her face reflecting his radiance because she herself could bring happiness to a little boy who found all too little of it in a world that was just too much for him.

Chapter Nine

IN SEPTEMBER, 1950, Margarete left us to go home to Germany to interpret the "American way" to her fellow countrymen. Even though it had taken a while for adjustments to be made on our part as well as hers, we had come to love her as our own, and she in turn loved us. After returning from the Church World Service Center in New Windsor,

Maryland, where I had taken Margarete to meet the other ninety-nine students who were also returning to their Fatherland, I felt completely exhausted and spent, mentally as well as physically. This may have accounted for some of the feelings I had the next few months, as we once again began to consider Stevie's welfare above everything else.

We had a tremendous apple harvest ahead of us, and because of the critical shortage of labor we felt that I could be of some help if we could make arrangements for the children. My youngest sister, who lived in a nearby city, agreed to come out and care for the children during the day and also prepare our noon and evening meals. This gave me time to assist Max at the packinghouse by answering the telephone, keeping the records on truck loadings, helping to wait on customers, keeping time records for our employees, and caring for the dozens of other small, irritating duties that would prevent him from giving the big ones his much-needed attention.

Nancy, my sister, had worked as an attendant in a hospital for mental defectives several summers before to help earn money for college expenses. Although she had worked with older persons, she had been with the retarded children enough to know and observe far more about them than an average person does. Because of her concern for Stevie, she had naturally been more interested in this problem while working there than she would have been otherwise. When she came out to be with us, we asked her to be very frank and if, after being with Stevie almost every day for more than two months, she felt that there were things we needed to know, to tell us, no matter how much it might hurt. Although Dr.

Black had been seeing him regularly for many months, and he had been seen by several other doctors and psychologists at various times in the past two years, we felt that seeing him every day in his home atmosphere would tell much that could not be seen in brief office interviews.

One day near the end of the harvest season, Max came back to work after lunch very late. I had finished eating and had gone back to start the packing operations at one o'clock. About two-thirty Max came in and quite casually, almost too casually, said: "Dotty, I was talking with Nancy at lunch, and she thinks that the doctors are not mistaken about Stevie. She told me that many of the little children where she worked at the institution in Maryland were just like him in many ways. She wonders if perhaps we ought to begin thinking in terms of finding a permanent home for Stevie for his own good as well as the good of our other three children."

I do not remember what I replied or what more he said at the moment, but I do recall the feeling of terrible unbridled hate and rage that swept over me for the next few moments. Like a small hurt child storming at the injustice of a cruel world, for a brief instant I hated everything and everybody, except Stevie. I felt that if I could only take him and go away —anywhere, from everything and everybody—the two of us could find happiness. The thought that anyone should suggest that he be taken from me was not to be borne for one moment. It was a possibility that had been lying dormant in our minds these many months, and now that we faced it in reality it caused the equivalent of a volcanic eruption in my emotions. The storm was over in a matter of seconds, and the tears which so often follow such an emotional upheaval began to spill from my eyes and choke my throat.

"Well, I wouldn't worry too much about it if I were you. They could *all* be mistaken, you know. We'll just take it easy for a while."

It was Max speaking again. I could hear the gentle reassurance of his voice above the clatter and noise made by the machinery and trucks, and I knew his eyes were filled with tenderness even though I could not see them through my tears.

I finished my work that afternoon as one moved by automatic controls. I could feel the thirty or more employees in the packinghouse looking at my stricken face, and I knew they probably wondered what could possibly have happened to me. From three o'clock on there were the usual customers. "Yes, this apple is best for frying. . . . No, that one isn't a very good apple for sauce; you need one that will cook up more. . . . Yes, we will be glad to ship a bushel to Florida for you; just give me the address and the variety you prefer. . . . Wait a minute, Walter, don't leave with that load on the truck until the invoice is written." All afternoon it went: people, telephone, papers to fill out, questions, apples, apples, apples. At last it was over and I went home.

For the first time in all the long weary months through which we had passed since that day in January nearly two years before, months in which we had alternated between hope and despair, I felt deep in my heart that our little son was destined to go through life without ever quite realizing what it was all about. With this realization came the knowledge that we would have to think of his future and the future of our other children in these terms. I knew that my sister was not a psychiatrist or a psychologist, knew that she could be mistaken by some chance, but I also knew that she was a very wise and discerning person and had observed Stevie in his home atmosphere long enough to be able to form a reasonably accurate opinion. We have always been thankful for those two months she spent with Stevie because, even though we trusted our doctors' judgment, yet being parents we were always sure that the doctors saw only Stevie's limitations, and those against a background that was strange and frightening to him.

Shortly after the apple harvest was over, at the suggestion of Dr. Black we took Stevie to our local Guidance Center for observation and testing. I shall never forget the compassionate personality we found in the psychologist at the Center who gave Stevie his tests. It is a strange thing how we parents come to know intuitively when psychologists and psychiatrists see us as human beings with real problems and not just as case histories for their little notebooks. (I must confess that after being probed and questioned I sometimes had the naughty desire to delve a bit into their own thinking to find out what they really believed about me and just how I would appear in one of their case histories!)

I never felt this way about Miss Mehus because I knew instinctively that she was a person who saw our problem as a human and an emotional one, not just another case history to be studied with the same cold analytical mind with which one would dissect a frog.

I told her of my sister's caring for Stevie for the past two months and the suggestion she had made that perhaps we should be thinking in terms of placing him in a home for retarded children at some future date. Miss Mehus pointed out some of the advantages of institutional care which to me seemed very logical ones, but she ended by assuring me that they did not like to suggest that a child be placed unless the parents themselves came to a belief that it was the wisest thing to do for all concerned. At that point she told me something for which I was totally unprepared—that often it took not months, but *years,* to secure placement for a child in a colony for the mentally defective. She also told me that our own State Training School was one of the best she had seen from the standpoint of cleanliness and physical care of the children, but that it did not rate very high in its training program because of lack of facilities and personnel.* She felt that if we were thinking at all about placing Stevie there, it would be wise to go through the necessary legal steps for commitment and then just wait for developments. We were assured that if by some chance Stevie should show remarkable improvement over a period of time and we should change

* In the intervening years since this interview with Miss Mehus the entire program of the State Department of Mental Hygiene and Hospitals has made tremendous progress under the leadership of two commissioners, Dr. Joseph E. Barrett and Dr. Hiram Davis. Physical facilities at the Lynchburg Training School and Hospital have been greatly expanded, and a comprehensive training program has been developed at the school through the dedicated efforts of two of its most recent superintendents, Dr. W. I. Prichard and Dr. Benedict Nagler.

our minds, we need not go through with the placement. All this seemed reasonable to me and also to Max when I told him of our conversation.

Dr. Black's opinion was concurrent with that of Miss Mehus; so in January of 1951 we went through the necessary legal procedure for Stevie's commitment to our Lynchburg State Training School and Hospital. This was the one step during our entire experience that I felt myself completely incapable of taking. When Dr. Black assured me it would not be necessary for me to be present at the legal commission, Max insisted that I not go, and in this one thing I took the easy way out.

At this time we were not completely sure in our own minds that this was the course we should follow. We felt it wise, however, to take the initial step, so that in event we arrived at such a conclusion, the period of waiting between our time of decision and the final break from home would not be such a long and heartbreaking one.

It is impossible to say just when, or at what point, we arrived in our thinking at the place where we believed that, for the good of all concerned, we should find another home for Stevie. It was a long, slow process. Many things entered into our thinking. I remembered two mental defectives whom I had known during childhood. Both were high-grade defectives, and both were mercilessly teased and tormented by the boys of the community. Each of them had spent a great deal of time in my own home, as Mother and Daddy had at all times been very compassionate and considerate toward them. One of the boys had worked for Daddy, and I remembered several times when in a fit of rage he would have committed murder had it not been for immediate intervention. No doubt the memory of those two lonely, pathetic figures played a part in my own thinking. I thought of the terrible and appalling loneliness of these children, the loneliness for a human companionship they could never quite find in a world which was beyond their comprehension. I tried to imagine just how I would feel, if quite suddenly I was transferred to a place where everyone had the mental capacity of an Einstein; and when I thought of what a constant sense of frustration that would be for me, it was easier to imagine how my own little boy must feel in a world of people with normal intellect.

Perhaps the strongest force to bear on our own problem was the constant fear that Stevie would severely hurt some smaller child. We not only had our own small daughter to think of but three children of my sister's, all of whom were younger than he, with whom he played much of the time. Many parents will deny vehemently that retarded children are dangerous to other children; they insist that their child would never hurt anyone. That is a generalization which is not applicable to all cases. Many retarded children are not dangerous, some even less so than average children; but it is not only useless but also foolish to deny the fact that a number of these children are potentially dangerous, not only to themselves but other children as well. I would agree that they are not intentionally so. In all his life I never saw Stevie do anything deliberately mean or unkind; in fact, most of the dangerous things he did were done in a mood of great joy and glee. Within a period of only a few months, three of his impetuous acts could easily have caused very serious injury or even death to my husband, our oldest son, and my sister's small baby. In every instance, although adults were present, because of the swift impulsiveness with which he moved, they would have been absolutely powerless to prevent what happened. Let me emphasize again that not *all* retarded children are likely to endanger the lives of other children, and in many instances some of them make wonderful playmates. But people who have worked in this field for many years will tell anyone that in certain types of retardation the element of danger is ever present because of quick, impulsive, irrational actions over which the child has little or no control.

I have talked with many parents of retarded children who sincerely believed that if they were only living in the country instead of a city their problem would end. It is true that the extra space, the quietness, contact with nature, and many other things present a definite advantage. However, on the modern-day farm where everything is highly mechanized there are many dangers present which are not present in an urban situation. Stevie was fascinated by everything electrical: motors, packinghouse machinery, the electric welder, the battery charger, household equipment. All these presented a constant source of danger as well as frustration to him, because he was not permitted to do precisely what he wished with them. Whereas many retarded children are content to sit passively and let the world go by, he filled his every waking moment with great activity; most of it was without any objective, and some of it was potentially harmful to his own well-being.

We tried to direct some of his ambition into useful channels. He learned to operate the can opener, and I often called him to open cans for me. But if I happened to be in another part of the house and he decided to open cans, it wasn't at all unusual to go into the kitchen and discover a neat row of cans on the cabinet with all the lids cut off, regardless of contents. That always resulted in a "Stevie-supper," which meant that we ate whatever it was that he happened to open. I often let him help me bake by beating eggs, but when he decided to begin adding ingredients, the results were sometimes disastrous and sometimes humorous. Once while mixing some cornbread, I had to leave the kitchen for a few minutes, and when I returned I found that Stevie had opened a can of chili con carne and poured the entire contents into my cornbread batter! Being a bit Scotch and a very great experimenter in the cooking line, I decided just to bake it anyhow. It was surprisingly good, and all of us had a good laugh and much praise for Stevie's chili con carne cornbread. These little episodes brought a light and welcome touch to an otherwise sad and tragic drama.

Another thing which influenced our decision to find another home for Stevie was his inability to enter into many of the family plans which our other children had a right to expect as part of their homelife. We took him to Sunday school until the difference in his behavior and that of the others became so pronounced that it disrupted the entire class. All of his teachers were wonderfully understanding and patient,

but we felt that it was an injustice to the teacher as well as
the other children to keep one child in the class who was not
able to understand what was taking place and who, because
he could not understand, became highly agitated and the center of attention for the other children. This caused a situation
almost impossible for instructing the class.

Here again is a problem which needs individual solution
in every case. Some retarded children can be taken into many
public places without serious disruption of attention, but
there are some for whom it is an absolute physical impossi-
bility to sit quietly for more than a few moments at a time.
Time and proper training will, in many cases take care of this,
but there are certain types of retardates for whom it seems
almost impossible to appear in public places without severe
embarrassment to themselves as well as others. Surely in
such cases we owe it to the child concerned to protect him
from needless suffering. It is very doubtful that what he
gains in knowledge and experience can ever quite compensate for what he loses in confidence and self-respect by being
made an object of either pity or derision.

I believe that possibly the thing which brought our thinking to a head, so to speak, was a very small, apparently in-
significant incident which happened the summer after we
had made our application in January. A friend came to call
on business for a few minutes, and his small daughter was
with him. She was several months older than Stevie. We were
standing just outside our packinghouse talking when Stevie
walked over and held out his hand to her as though he wanted
to have her come play with him. She took hold of her father's

hand and shrank back behind his legs with real terror in her little eyes; she was *afraid* of Stevie! I think that it was not because she believed he would hurt her but because here was a little boy who was different; here was a little boy almost her age who couldn't even talk; something was *wrong,* and because the little girl couldn't *understand,* she *feared.* Had she been a shy, bashful child, her reaction would not have been surprising, but she was accustomed to playing with little boys, and it was not a look of normal little-girl shyness I saw in her face but one of real terror.

That was only one time. There were others, many of them, when I saw that even though the children made a very real effort to include Stevie in their fun and help him fit into their little world, it always ended in defeat for them and absolute frustration for him. Many times a child would stand and look at him with the penetrating, candid gaze only a small child can give, then turn to me and say: "Well, what's the *matter* with Stevie? What makes him act like that?" The wounded and hurt look in his beautiful brown eyes so stabbed my heart that I soon came to the conclusion that anything would be better than this, better than seeing him lonely, hurt, rejected, not because his playmates were unkind but because they lived in a world which would forever be denied to him, a world which could be unlocked only by that one invaluable key called intellect.

There was another vital and final element which helped us decide what to do. I had been taught to believe, and so had Max, that every decision one faced should be made in the light of what Jesus, as our human interpreter of God, would do in a given situation. Because there was no exact parallel to our problem given in the record of his life, it would have been impossible to say that he would or would not follow a particular course. In our search for an answer to this question the only conclusion we could come to was that he would do that thing which in his judgment was most *merciful,* most *kind,* and would *cause the least suffering to the child* itself regardless of what it might cost the parents in mental anguish and sorrow.

Stevie was not happy with us, and we knew it; our other children were facing problems which were becoming bigger as the months went by; our home life was suffering from the strain of having to give so much time to the actual physical care and training of our little son that no time was left for the many small joys which the other children had a right to expect. If it is an admission of defeat—that I was not big enough, or not wise enough, or not courageous enough to create a reasonably satisfactory life for the six of us in the face of all the personalities and issues involved—then I must admit to the fact. For a long while I suffered greatly from this sense of frustration, of failure to meet a situation which I thought I should surely be able to meet. But as I look back now I wonder if it would not have led to a greater defeat, a greater failure, if I had clung tenaciously to the belief that I was equal to the challenge before me.

And so it was that as the weeks lengthened into months, the conviction grew within both of us that for Stevie's sake, for the sake of our other three children, the most merciful thing, the kindest thing, would be to permit Stevie to find a home among those who, like himself, would live forever in the land of childhood.

Chapter Ten

By the fall of 1951 we had passed through the various cycles in which most parents of retarded children seem to move: first utter disbelief, then gradual acceptance, and finally an overwhelming desire to *do* something about the entire problem. We became literally obsessed with the feeling that we must make an effort to help improve the prevailing conditions not only for our own child but for other children and parents in future generations.

Early in 1951 an article appeared in *Better Homes and Gardens* magazine entitled "Not Quite Bright." It was the first article pertaining to our problem I had found in a national publication. Shortly afterward a story in the *Christian Herald* told of the organization of a parent group in Chicago and their subsequent founding of a day school for retarded

children. Both these articles made reference to the National
Association for Retarded Children, an organization whose
purpose was to bring concrete help and assistance to retarded
children and their parents. A short time later the poignant
and tender story of Pearl Buck's retarded daughter was published in *Ladies' Home Journal* under the title "The Child
Who Never Grew." This also gave recognition to the work of
the national organization. By this time my interest was so
thoroughly aroused that I wanted to know more about the
NARC and the forming of local councils, but the day-by-day
struggle of trying to meet the needs and problems arising in
my own home prevented me from taking any definite steps.

In September, Mrs. James, the teacher with whom I had
talked about Stevie, telephoned me late one afternoon and
asked me if we would be interested in joining with other
parents in our area to form an association for working in the
interest of our children. I told her of reading these articles
and of our interest. She informed me that the first meeting
would be held that very evening. Max and I immediately
canceled other plans for the evening in order that we might
attend.

It would be impossible to describe just how we parents
felt that first evening. All of us had belonged to various organizations, but this was the first one with which we had
ever been affiliated which required that we literally go through
a Gethsemane before being eligible for membership. We were
a little shy with one another at first, somewhat hesitant about
how to proceed, perhaps even a bit overwhelmed to sit in the
presence of such a large number who had known terrific men-

tal strain and heartache. There were several present who had become acquainted through their mutual problem, but most of us were total strangers to one another.

We soon found that our hostess, Mrs. Waid, was blessed with a gentle and rare capacity for making people feel comfortable, and in a short time all our reserve was broken. Soon we were all wanting to talk with the others. And what did we talk about? Our *children,* of course! We were all impressed with the pathetic eagerness with which we shared our problems. It was truly a blessed relief to sit down and talk with someone who really understood. Although many of us had most understanding families, friends, and neighbors, yet we knew that they could share our grief in only a very limited way.

We were surprised to see that the fathers were just as eager to talk "children" as the mothers were. Very often in a mixed gathering the fathers talk shop while the mothers talk about their children and homes, but in all parent councils for retarded children the fathers seem just as glad to have someone to talk to about their children as the mothers do. A number of the fathers were businessmen, and a few had met before in this capacity, but not one of them knew that any of the others was the father of a retarded child. At our third meeting a member was amazed to see his Sunday school teacher join the group. Neither of them knew the other had been carrying this burden in his heart.

After several preliminary meetings in which we were learning to know one another better, our officers were elected and a projects committee was appointed. This committee met and made plans for the year's work. These were presented at the following meeting:

1. That we sponsor a series of radio programs with a two-fold purpose:
   a. To acquaint the public with the aims and purposes of the council.
   b. To provide general information to an unenlightened public about the age-old problems of mental deficiency and mental illness.
2. That a legislative committee be appointed to study every phase of legal provision within our state relative to the mentally retarded, with the idea of helping to bring about future legislation for the betterment of these children.
3. That a committee be appointed to secure information relative to our State Training School to share with the parents, and also try to ascertain ways in which such a group as ours could be helped to this state institution.
4. That two parties be planned for our children, most of whom were denied the social privileges of normal children.

These four projects were unanimously adopted, and before the year was over we had done something about every one of them.

We soon discovered that even though many of our problems were the same, yet our children were of all types, grades, and degrees of retardation, and the needs of each were somewhat different. We realized before long that to work together most effectively for the betterment of these children, each of us would have to lose something of his or her own individual problem. When each began to plan and think in terms of *all* retarded children rather that just his own child, worthwhile things began to happen. We had little concrete help to guide us in those beginning days, as the national organization was still in its infancy, struggling with the problems of policy, of insufficient funds, of all the many other details that arise to harass any organization devoted to the welfare of humanity. So, like the proverbial fools rushing in where angels fear to tread, we plunged ahead with our own plans and ideas. Since I had had some very limited experience in writing, and both Max and I had done some public speaking, we were appointed to the publicity committee for our newly formed association.

Realizing that inviting persons to become members of such an organization was in itself a rather delicate problem, we decided that it would be good if we could have a radio program which would explain the aims and purposes of the organization. We felt this would be an impersonal way to reach many parents who needed our help. The manager of our largest radio station, WDBJ, was a personal friend of my family; so we decided to ask him if time could be made available for such a program, and if so, how much cost would be involved. He introduced me to Mr. Reynolds, the program manager of the station, whom we found to be most interested in what we were trying to do in behalf of this problem. Mr. Reynolds not only offered to give us time for a fifteen-minute program but suggested that the station would be glad to give us time for a three-month series of programs for the

purpose of educating the public as to the actual truth about
the subjects of mental deficiency and mental illness. He believed, along with us, that if the general public understood
the truth about mental abnormalities many of the so-called
problems could be eliminated for the families of those suffering from mental ailments.

I left the radio station that day almost overwhelmed. Having gone in expecting to pay for one fifteen-minute program,
I came out with not only one, but the possibility for thirteen
more on free time. At our next parent meeting the members
enthusiastically accepted the idea as a worthwhile project.
The next question to arise was: "Who will write the scripts
and do the programs?" Mr. Reynolds had pointed out that
even though they would be glad to furnish the radio time,
his staff would not be able to give any help in preparation of
the program material. It seemed that none of the other members were any more qualified for such an undertaking than
we were, so Max and I promised that in some way the publicity committee would see the job through.

I went home from that meeting and lay awake until five
o'clock in the morning in a state of mental turmoil. Max very
sensibly went to sleep! More than once in the days that followed I was tempted to telephone the program manager and
tell him that for once in my life I had committed myself to a
task I just couldn't see through. The temptation to forget
about the entire matter was an overwhelming one, but the
faces of the mentally retarded haunted me day and night, and
the thought returned to me over and over that here at last was
an opportunity to do something constructive about the situa-

tion. True, it was a small thing, but it could be a beginning toward creating a more sympathetic and understanding world for the retarded and their families.

We knew intuitively that such a series of programs had the possibility of doing more harm than good if not written and presented with the utmost discretion, so we began by seeking help and advice from people we knew were qualified to give it. A letter to Dr. Joseph E. Barrett, our State Mental Hygiene Commissioner, brought the reply that he not only thought the idea a worthwhile one but that he would be happy to advise and assist us in any way possible. Letters to other individuals brought similar replies; and we began to feel that even though we had plunged into a terrific task, we at least would have plenty of moral support.

Shortly after the Christmas holidays of that year our small dining room began to look like an official library on mental deficiency! We chose to write at the dining room table because both our desks were filled with personal and business necessities, and by setting up our writing shop in the dining room it could remain undisturbed from day to day. We left the bright red holiday tablecloth on the table, thinking it would bring a note of color and cheer to the difficult and somewhat gloomy task ahead of us. But it was soon buried beneath stacks of pamphlets, books, scratch pads, paper, and numerous copies of the *American Journal of Mental Deficiency*. We made a trip to our state capitol at Richmond to talk with our Mental Hygiene Commissioner. Dr. Barrett was warmly sympathetic toward our newly organized parent council and the radio program, and he was also deeply interested in our own personal problem. He gave us much helpful advice in outlining our series of programs and also another armload of reading material, including one of his own manuscripts. One of his assistants, Mrs. Helen Smith Mugler, Educational Director of the Department of Mental Hygiene and Hospitals, also gave us advice and encouragement. It was she who later checked each manuscript we wrote for scientific accuracy.

While in Richmond we went over to the State Library to call on a friend of ours who served as head of the Extension Department. We told her why we were in Richmond, and she immediately found a book for me which she thought could be of great value to one who had never written a radio script before. Although the book had been written primarily for library publicity purposes, it contained invaluable suggestions about radio script writing technique in general. From this book we obtained much of the necessary know-how to tackle the job which we would not have attempted under any circumstances six months before.

For the next three months, every minute of my spare time (and much of it that was not *spare!*) was devoted to digesting this mountain of material we had collected and getting it into a listenable form. Heaven surely smiled upon us during those three months, because all of us escaped the usual winter epidemic of influenza and colds. The children were unusually cooperative, and even little Stevie seemed to realize that Mother was doing some important work because he caused a minimum number of problems. Most of the actual writing was done while the children were in bed for their afternoon naps or at night and very early in the morning before they were out of bed.

Although I did the writing of the scripts, Max offered invaluable suggestions as to rephrasing certain ideas or sentences to make them more pleasing to the ear, or more clear and concise. The spoken idea and the written idea are two different things entirely, and I had constantly to struggle with the fact that what looked good and registered properly when read could be entirely lost when presented orally, particularly by the indirect medium of radio. Each fifteen-minute script had to be written, read, and reread many times to obtain the proper clarity, absolute accuracy, and split-second timing.

It is impossible to describe how we felt the last few mintues prior to that first broadcast in April, 1952. We knew there would be many people who would sadly misunderstand our motive in bringing such a well-hidden problem into the open. We knew that to many it would appear unthinkable that we, the parents of a retarded child, should, so to speak, broadcast the fact in an effort to increase understanding of the problem by the general populace. In my own mind I could well imagine what many people would be saying, and most of it wasn't very flattering to my ego either; but like Francis of Assisi, we had come to the place where we no longer sought to be understood, but to understand.

Several subsequent programs included interviews with professional men whose work involved contact with the mentally defective and their families. One program was devoted entirely to answering questions sent in by the radio audience; two local psychiatrists and a social worker from the Guidance Center served as a panel to answer these questions. Two programs were prepared and presented by the chairman of our legislative committee relative to the need for special educational facilities for retarded children. The climax of our series came with the presentation of a recorded interview with Pearl S. Buck, which was intended primarily as a message of encouragement to parents with retarded children. I had written to her and explained what we were attempting to do, and she most graciously consented to grant an interview which could be recorded for our series of programs. Pearl Buck's magnificent spirit was evident in every word she spoke to these parents whose problems she understood so well from her own experience.

The therapeutic value to us as parents of a retarded child in arranging and presenting this series of radio programs was beyond description. As I reflect upon it now, it seems almost providential that this work came at just the time it did because it was during this period that Stevie left us to make his home in a new world. As we read and studied and found the truth about so many things, a very definite healing began to take place because we could now begin to look at this problem with our heads as well as our hearts. A statement by Elsie Castendyck in her excellent book *The Handicapped Child* brought to my attention a fact which should be engraved on the minds of every person with a retarded child: "There is no substitute for adequate factual information and clear scientific explanation as a means of counteracting the tendency to indulge in random emotional concern in this, as in any other, disquieting situation." It is true that this is a problem about which there are still a great many unanswered questions, but unfortunately many, many parents have made little effort to carefully study the facts that are reasonably certain. Although in the past there has been a real dearth of literature for the parents of retarded children, this condition is rapidly changing, and there is no real reason now for any parent to be totally uninformed about this problem.

We have reason to believe that our efforts were of value not only to ourselves but to others as well, because for months we met people who, with tears in their eyes, told us of how they had been helped by hearing some specific program. It had cost us much—much in time, much in emotion, much in sheer hard work, much in pride—but, as always, the reward was far greater than the cost, because this was done from our hearts in the belief that it was a real service to the most pathetic and misunderstood of God's human creatures, the mentally defective child.

Chapter Eleven

NEAR THE MIDDLE of February, while we were thoroughly engrossed in the work of writing our radio scripts, a letter arrived for us from our State Training School. I had been corresponding with Dr. Hammer, one of the staff members, about one of our radio programs and naturally supposed that the letter would be from him. Upon opening it, we found it to be a brief letter from the superintendent informing us that Stevie could be accepted as a patient the last week in February. It was like the proverbial bolt from the blue; we had been told only a short time before while visiting the school that it would probably be the middle of the summer before he could be accepted. This notice gave us only two weeks in which to prepare his clothes and steel our own courage to the point necessary for carrying out the decision we had reached after months and years of agonizing over it. For months I had been storing in my mind and heart every precious moment we shared together as a family, realizing that all too soon Stevie would not be with us to enjoy the little he could as a member of our family. Now that the time was only two weeks away the moments when all four of the children were together at one time were so painfully poignant that I believed at times I could not bear it. It was good that I had to work—good that every minute was so filled that there was little time left for miring down in self-pity.

Although there was little our family and friends could do in a tangible way, we knew that all of them were remembering us daily that we might have the necessary physical stamina and spiritual courage to face what was before us. A letter from one on my older sisters, who was a missionary in India, came at a strategic time to give me comfort. She wrote: "Every time there has been a major crisis to face in my own life I've always gained strength in this one thought, *This is only temporary.* Just remember that everything about life is only temporary, nothing is final, and it will give you the necessary boost to meet many of life's most crushing experiences."

One *can* bear almost anything if he believes it is only temporary, and I found it a lifesaving philosophy during those last days. Even though we realized that in all probability a great part of Stevie's allotted span of years on this earth would be spent away from us, it was comforting to remember that life here on earth is, after all, only temporary, and that in the life beyond we would have the great, unimaginable joy of seeing our little son as God would like all his children to be, whole and perfect in every detail.

We had talked with our older children many times about the possibility that the time might come when it would be necessary for Stevie to go live in another home where there were other little boys just like himself. Even though we had talked about it before, the news that he would go very soon brought a sad scene for all of us. I shall never forget holding Andy on my knee and trying to explain through his tears, and my own, that even though Stevie was a part of our family, sometimes families must be divided for the good of all concerned. The thought that Stevie had to be denied the privilege of continuing as part of our family was just too much for Andy's tender little heart. After we explained that Stevie would have many opportunities for training at the State School that he would never have if he stayed with us, the children seemed reconciled to the fact that he would just be "going away to school" instead of staying at home and going to school as they did. We assured them that Stevie could come to visit us and we would go to visit him, so he would still be a part of our family even though he did not make his home with us.

The day of his going dawned bright and warm. My sister (who was married to Max's brother). and her husband offered to go with us—and we did not refuse their going. Together we had shared the happiest moments of our lives; together we would face this time of parting, for their grief over this child was almost as deep as our own. Grandfather and Grandmother Murray came to the car to kiss Stevie goodbye, and we think he must have believed it strange indeed to see not only his mother and daddy, Uncle Kent and Aunt Miriam, but Grandmother and Grandfather as well with tears streaming down their faces. Although we had told him for several days that "Stevie's is going to go to a new home," there was apparently no realization on his part as to just what was taking place.

There are no words to describe the feelings through which parents go as they bid their child good-bye, as they leave him in a home for the mentally defective. I will make no attempt to do so. But there is one point I would like to try to make for the benefit of those people who work in such institutions. For years I had imagined, when I thought of it at all, that employees in mental institutions would be brusque, efficient, and probably completely indifferent to the feelings of families who must leave their loved ones in such homes. To the everlasting credit of the employees at our Lynchburg Training School, both my husband and I can say that we at no time ever received anything but the most kind and sympathetic consideration. We had been there several times before we took Stevie to stay and had talked with a number of the employees and also to many of the patients. Although there may have been situations which, to an inexperienced and uninformed person may have seemed to be far from ideal, yet we never at any time saw any indication that the patients were ill-treated. It always seemed to us that, considering the restricted facilities with which they had to work and the very limited personnel, they were doing a good job.

There were two people who helped us through the heart-rending experience of that day to whom my gratitude will be unending. One was the nurse who received Stevie into the hospital for inoculations and observation. The other was one of the patients who worked in the hospital. I do not remember the nurse's name, but I do remember her beautiful brown eyes and her compassion as she asked me questions for filling out the preliminary report on Stevie.

We had answered all the usual questions one answers when leaving a child in the care of any hospital, and then came one for which I was totally unprepared.

"Mrs. Murray, are there any little things you would like to tell me about Stevie that would make it easier for him in making his adjustment here—any little peculiarities or obsessions that we should know about, so that we can try to do for him just as you have been doing at home as nearly as possible?" she asked.

"Why, yes," I said. "There are many little things that are very important to him, but we didn't expect that you should even try to observe them here where there are so many to care for."

I tried to tell her, tried to explain some of the small details which loom so large to the retarded child, details which mothers observe to make them happy and to give them security, but it was too much for me, and my sister finished while I sat sobbing as though my heart would break. She told of our family custom of holding hands around the table for mealtime prayer, a custom so important to Stevie that though we were out in the woods on a picnic we must still hold hands or he would neither eat nor pray. There were others— food likes and dislikes, bedtime prayers, many foolish little quirks that the mothers of such children are sure no one else in all the world will understand or make allowance for.

"You see, they are the things we really want to know, and we will do them whenever possible to give your child a feeling of security as he changes from one way of life to another," she said.

The interview was over, and we were ready to go. We kissed Stevie good-bye, and by now he seemed to sense that something most unusual was happening. He was very pale

and looked at the four of us with his big brown eyes as
though to say, "Well, you aren't going without *me,* are you?"
It was then that Clyde came and put his arm about Max's
shoulder. Clyde was a patient at the hospital, a mental defective, to be sure, but with the wisdom of the ages in his
heart.

"Now don't you all be worryin' none 'bout your little boy
not gettin' enough lovin'," he said gently. "I loves little children and I've always loved them all my life, and there ain't
no little child 'round here go need for any lovin' as long as
I'm around."

The busy doctors and nurses with their heads filled with
technical knowledge scurried about attending to their duties,
but it was Clyde, poor childlike Clyde, who knew instinctively
the thing we most needed to hear as we turned away from
our little son and left him in the hands of others who from
now on would minister to him in our stead. We knew that
though the staff at the hospital would meet his physical needs,
the most important need of all would be met by Clyde, and
many others like him, who would give Stevie the "lovin' "
that was as necessary to his well-being as sunshine is to
flowers.

Chapter Twelve

WE WENT HOME to plunge into work, work, work. I knew that the sudden release from the watchful care which had become so much a part of my life for the past four years could easily provide me with the time to have a real breakdown, both physically and mentally. For a period of time I worked too hard, driving myself almost beyond human endurance, but I now believe it was the means of saving myself. Our radio programs were scheduled to begin the first week in April and were to run through June. I kept telling myself over and over: "Now you can't let up until all these programs are finished; if you must collapse from the strain you've been through, just wait until July before you do it." That was most ridiculous, and I knew it, but it worked, and, by the time July arrived, other things had arisen which made me think there still wasn't the necessary time to collapse! If this sounds a bit facetious, it is not intended as such. I am not foolish enough to believe that a nervous breakdown is a laughing matter, or that one could always be prevented by such an unorthodox method. I do believe, however, that there is real merit to the idea of becoming so wrapped up in a cause that we forget ourselves, because often while we are bending our energies toward helping others, a healing comes for our own overwrought and overworked bodies and minds.

We went to see Stevie frequently during those first few

months. There was some doubt in our minds about how soon
our children should go, but they insisted on going the first
time, and we took them with us, although they could not see
Stevie, since he was still on the hospital ward. I dreaded this
visit almost as much as taking him in the first place, and it
was hard. He looked pale and very thin, and as we saw him
with all the other patients in the hospital ward, we were
struck anew with the fact that now Stevie was really one of
them. At first sight of us he did not seem to realize just who
we were, but when we called his name and began to talk to
him a flicker of recognition came immediately to his eyes. We
sat with him for a few minutes, and talked with some of the
other patients and also the nurse. The nurse assured us he
seemed to be making the adjustment very well. She felt that
his pale look came partly from the series of injections he had
been receiving which were necessary for all patients coming
into the institution. Just before leaving I gave him a box
filled with macaroni beads for stringing and a few other small
trinkets. He began stringing beads and when we said, "Bye,
Stevie, we'll be back," he continued to string beads and re-
peated after us as was his little custom, "Bye, Stevie." The
hospital authorities assured us that we were welcome to come
at any time.

Other visits were much the same. Even though he seemed
happy to see us, he was not seemingly too disturbed when
we left, because we always told him we would be back soon.
And I think that somehow he knew we would. Very soon
the boys on his ward began to anticipate our visits as much
as, or, in some cases, even more than Stevie did. Part of it

was undoubtedly due to the fact that there were often bubble-gum and apples to be had when Stevie's mother and daddy came. But in addition to that they were just overjoyed to have someone from the outside to visit their ward. We learned that very frequently children are placed in an institution and then utterly ignored by their families. As I learned to know other parents in our area who had children there, I would frequently go to call on their children for a few minutes. One little fellow always greets me with "Did you see my mommy?" His mother lives more than two hundred miles from me, but because I would tell some other little boy of seeing his own mother, this particular little fellow believes that I should have seen his mommy also.

We brought Stevie home for a week during the summer after he had been there since February. He seemed quite happy to get back to his home, but was equally as happy to get back to the school with the boys and his favorite attendant, Keezee. We had to take him back to the hospital for a routine checkup before he could go back on his ward. He was some-what frightened at being left in the hospital again, but when we saw Clyde sitting in a rocking chair with a pitiful little infant in his arms, rocking it as tenderly as any mother could ever have done, we knew that Stevie would be well looked after during his stay on the hospital ward. We brought him home again at Christmas, and it was the happiest Christmas we had experienced in several years. Stevie had lost much of the nervous drive which had caused him to be so terrifically destructive while he had been living with us. We feel now that many of the problems we had with him came as a result of his not being able to cope with a world that to him was too confusing and frustrating. He had been just striking out in hurt resentment at a world which he could not understand, and which in turn could not understand him. The simplified life at the institution and the patient and sympathetic efforts of a psychologist whom Stevie loved dearly were beginning to bear some fruit.

One morning after Stevie had been gone for several months our small daughter, who was then four and one-half years old, looked up at me from the floor where she was playing with her dolls. "Mamma," she said, "are you glad Stevie doesn't live here at our house anymore?" At first I was so astonished I could scarcely think, as we had not even mentioned Stevie's name that particular morning. Not knowing how to answer her, I said: "Well, I'm not so sure. Are *you* glad Stevie doesn't live here at our home anymore?" She answered without a moment's hesitation: "Yes, I'm glad Stevie has gone to live at his other home."

For a moment I was so stunned at what seemed to be her utter callousness that I could not think, and then I began to ask myself some questions. After all, why shouldn't she be glad when for the first time within her memory she could sit down and play in peace without having her favorite doll's eyes punched out or, worse yet, having it thrown into the fireplace, or being afraid to climb on the stairs or slicky-slide for fear Stevie in a sudden impetuous movement would shove her off. Could one blame one so young for being happy over the natural birthright of every child to play without constant interruption from another who was incapable of joining in that play? As I looked long and carefully (and I hope truthfully) into the reactions of not only this smallest child, but the other children, and also my husband and myself, it could not be denied that we were truly living in a different world as far as our homelife was concerned. As I thought of Stevie's visits with us and his return to the "other home," I could not help but wonder if perhaps he himself might not be glad that "Stevie doesn't live at our home anymore." There may be those who will read this statement and not be able to comprehend that such a situation could or should exist, but those who have worked in this field a number of years will know precisely what I mean.

On February 19, 1953, Stevie was eight years old. I went to the State School along with two mothers of our Roanoke Council for Retarded Children to help him celebrate his birthday with a party for all the boys on his ward. The attendant had placed a table, covered with a white cloth, in the center of their playroom. Stevie was placed at the head of the table as the guest of honor. The cake which Anne had so beautifully and lovingly decorated for him was placed in the center of the table. Cookies, chewing gum, apples, and cider were provided for each eager little boy.

Stevie's eyes shone like stars as he looked at his birthday cake with the eight burning candles. The two attendants, the mothers, and all the little boys who could joined in singing the happy birthday song. It was small wonder that the three mothers arrived at the last note with choked voices and eyes bright from unshed tears. We served the refreshments, cleaned up the crumbs, cups, and paper, and prepared to leave.

Leave-taking was still very hard after an entire year; I think it will always be so, but there is no easy road, no life without suffering, for the parents of a retarded child, whether we have them with us or away from us.

We left Stevie sitting on the steps happily blowing bubbles from a jar of Bubble-O I had given him as I kissed him good-bye and assured him we would come again. The sight of his happy little eyes eagerly following each bubble as he blew them into the fading winter twilight stabbed my heart with both joy and pain, pain that he was no longer wholly our own, but joy that he had found happiness, because Stevie was now truly home at last, at home among those who lived in the kind of world which he could understand and be happy in.

As we drove through the school grounds to the outside world, several of the older patients, as was their custom, waved and called good-bye to us. All three of us were unashamedly weeping, and the tables must have been turned on us that day, for from the looks on their faces when they saw our tears I am sure that some of those patients must have turned to another to say "Well, what's the matter with *them*—why do they act that way?"

PART II

Chapter Thirteen

EVEN THOUGH we have not faced the problem of a retarded child in the family as long as many people have, we have learned enough from our experience to have some general observations which we believe worthy of sharing with others.

If by some magic formula a serum could be developed which could be administered to the parents of a mentally retarded child for their comfort, do you know what I believe it shoud be? *It should be one which would give them complete immunity to the pressure of public opinion.* On the surface this may sound a bit facetious, but when we probe deeply into our own thinking, isn't a very large part of our hurt, our question of what to do or not to do, much of our real problem itself, due to the pressure of public opinion? Whether we do or do not have guilt complexes, one of our first reactions when we face the fact that we are the parents of a retarded child is: "What will people think?" We imagine just what our friends, relatives, and neighbors are saying and thinking because they have discovered that we are the parents of a mentally crippled child. Not one of us will deny that they probably do say and think certain things, but, after all, how much does it *really* matter? How much should we let it hurt us? Or, how much should public opinion affect important decisions we must make in regard to the child's welfare? Max brought an observation to my attention shortly after we came face to face with this realization in our own experience.

"You know, Dotty," he said one night after we had been talking about the problems this new development posed within our family, "all this seems rather dreadful now, and I guess we are doing a lot of foolish wondering about what people are thinking and saying. But do you realize that after the initial shock wears off they just won't think much at all? Everyone will be too busy worrying about his own problems and griefs to give very much thought to our own."

This is a very obvious conclusion but one which I believe worth pointing out. Think of your own reaction after hearing a bit of startling news. For a few days, perhaps even a week, you may give some thought to it, but unless it concerns you or your immediate family, very soon you are so involved in thinking about your own problems that the other scarcely enters your mind. Then, too, it has always been a belief of mine that those people who do not have enough of their own daily affairs to keep them well occupied are ones whose opinions about my own should make little difference to me. Unless we as parents of retarded children make a very conscious effort to rise above being affected too much by what people will think, we may find ourselves floundering in a morass of despair from which it is all but impossible to extricate ourselves.

Another thing which we believe valuable for parents of retarded children to know is this: *For a certain period of time after we face this problem in its initial stages, we are totally incapable of being completely rational about it.* Do not be alarmed and think I am indicating that our own mental powers are affected by the lack in our child; but we should understand that after any extreme emotional shock we are not our normal selves. Someone has wisely observed: "There are two women who should never be judged for their actions, one in great sorrow, one in love." The implication is that in the grip of either extreme emotion we cannot truly follow our normal pattern of thinking. For some people this period of readjustment back to normalcy after an emotional shock is a comparatively short one and can be accomplished without too much pain. Some parents of retarded children can come to such complete acceptance within a few years that they can once again think in somewhat the same pattern as they thought before this sorrow came to them. For others it takes much longer, and there may even be those who are never able to see life again as good and worth living.

Any great emotional shock simply does something to our thought pattern which makes it necessary for us to have a period of time for recovery. Of course, we are never precisely the same again, but after a few years have passed, most of us can think and reason in more rational terms than in our initial grief. If we are truly honest with ourselves, most of us can look back and remember times when our deep resentment against some doctor or perhaps even a friend, neighbor, or relative was not justified at all but came about because we were still in a state of emotional shock in which our feelings were somewhat on edge. In the deep recesses of our memory, probably many of us have stored wounds and hurts inflicted upon us during this period. We would do well to wipe them out completely—forget about them entirely—instead of bringing them out to review over and over so that they will always remain with us. The inevitable result in retaining such memories will be a bitter and warped personality. It is the universal cry of parents of retarded children that the "public just doesn't understand," and that statement is true, every word of it. But in our accusation against the public let us each remember that only a few years ago *we* were a part of that same uncomprehending public, and perhaps with our own lack of information we may have been guilty of unintentionally wounding another parent.

These are not statements of accusation against the parents of retarded children, and we hope they will not·be interpreted as such; they are only a plea for growth on our part to the extent that we make some attempt to understand the attitude of the misinformed public as well as helping the parents to understand themselves better. We cannot expect to change quickly the attitudes and ideas about any situation which have been accumulating for centuries. Of one thing I am sure, however: We will never gain the kind of compassionate understanding we are seeking for our children until the bitterness in our own hearts is overcome.

During the initial period of severe emotional distress there is always the grave danger of a strained relationship between the parents of a retarded child. Each in his own anguish of heart may secretly be placing the responsibility for the child's condition on the other. Then, too, there will almost surely be times when there will be disagreement as to what course should be followed as far as discipline is concerned. One parent will sometimes be oversolicitious in the eyes of the other. This, in reverse, may make the one who may not be seem harsh and cruel toward the child.

Even if there are no differences between the parents, just the physical and mental weariness which arises from the daily care of a retarded child can create a strain in marriage which, if not properly understood, can lead to greater grief and sorrow. Adjustments must be made in any marriage, but where a retarded child is involved and the feelings and emotions of each parent are going through an abnormal phase, every effort should be made on the part of each to understand the feelings and emotions of the other. I have been told by authorities in this field that it is not at all uncommon for parents, either one or both, to develop a genuine feeling of revulsion or hatred for their child. Parents should by all means seek expert help when the emotional storm through which they are passing causes them to feel this way. Often parents will feel so guilty when this is the case that it is very difficult for them to take their problem to someone for help, but under the guidance of a wise psychiatrist they may soon discover the reasons for their seemingly "un-parent-like" feeling.

All of us are likely to have feelings and emotions during this period which we need to understand better if we are to control them properly and use them for our own spiritual growth. For those parents who are successful in weathering this storm of adjustment together, the rewards are great. In every case the marriage bonds are more real, and they are closer than ever because of their mutual suffering.

Another most obvious need for parents of retarded children is the time for recreation or some absorbing interest that can be turned to for relief from the tension built up by living and working under an emotionl strain. Here again one has to face the frightening bugaboo of public opinion, but for our own good this is one field in which it should be completely ignored. In the initial stages of our grief many of us lose interest in everything. Occupations which we enjoyed before and which were an important part of our lives suddenly seem useless, senseless, and a complete waste of time and energy. For our own good we need actually to force ourselves, if necessary, to do something which will take our minds away from our child, and ourselves for a short time daily.

In my own case I believe that my music was the means of saving me from more serious emotional damage. My mother was a music teacher, as was also an older sister; so I had been surrounded by music since my earliest memory. I had played the piano from my childhood, and when the opportunity presented itself to study pipe organ so that I could be of greater service to my church, I immediately took advantage of it, although it was not an easy thing to accomplish with my home and four children to care for. Only a few months of study had gone by when our suspicions about Stevie were confirmed. Much of my practice was done from five to seven o'clock in the morning before the children were awake, but I did take one entire afternoon each week for practice while the faithful Birdie cared for the children.

I am quite sure that had it not been for my husband, my mother, the doctor, and my organ teacher, I would have followed my first impulse to give it up completely so that I could devote my entire time to Stevie and the other children. My teacher pointed out the therapeutic value of music in itself, and the doctor assured me that I would be far better off to maintain an interest in something outside my home and family, if my physical strength were equal to it. The study was most difficult for me, as it had been many years since I had worked in music with any real diligence. For many weary months the dissonant sounds I made on the organ reminded me of my own inner struggle and conflict. But gradually, as time went on, my hands, feet, and brain began to coordinate to the extent that it was possible for me to create sounds which more nearly resembled music!

As I look back now I often wonder if I would have had the fortitude to stay by it long enough to achieve any worthwhile results had it not been for the inner compulsion of grief which drove me relentlessly. Many times after an unusually difficult practice I wet those organ keys with tears of sheer emotional release. I had a little private joke with myself that I couldn't be quite sure whether they were tears resulting from the unceasing ache in my heart or the dreadful noises I had made! But at least they served a useful purpose, and I

always went home with a new lease on life after spending
those hours at the organ in a quiet church. The patience, understanding, and kindness of my teacher were a great motivat-
ing force in helping me to keep going when the struggle
seemed almost humanly impossible.

A dear friend of mine found her release in bird study and
garden club work, and she has achieved a place of preemi-
nence in both. These hobbies had the added advantage of
being ones which could in a very large measure be shared
with her retarded son. Many mothers are prone to believe
so intently that the children must come first that they refuse to
take any time for their own personal development; but all
mothers need some time for themselves, and it is my own
belief that mothers of retarded children need this far more
than those of normal children. Because of the extreme de-
pendence of our retarded children, it is easy for us to become
so devoted to their care that we believe no one can care for
them other than ourselves. For the good of the child itself,
we need to realize that another person should be able to care
for it in an emergency, or to provide a few hours' relief each
week for the benefit of the mother.

There is one phase of the problem of mental retardation
which is completely different today from what it was when
we first faced the problem with our own little son. This has
come about primarily because of the efforts of the National
Association for Retarded Children. When we first became
aware of Stevie's mental limitation, I asked our physician
if there was not something I could read which would help
me to understand more about this entire situation, something

which would help me not only to deal more wisely with Stevie but to understand myself as well. There was absolutely nothing for him to recommend to me. I discovered later that there were a few technical books prepared for those who worked with retarded children professionally, but for the help of parents there seemed to be nothing—at least not where we could find it. Since that time, through the efforts of the NARC, much helpful literature in the form of small brochures and booklets has appeared. A number of informative books have also been written, aimed at helping the parents.

This brings me to the fourth point which I believe to be absolutely essential in making a successful adjustment: *Inform yourself as to the actual truth about mental retardation.* "Ye shall know the truth, and the truth shall make you free." In no area of life can this be more applicable than in the area of either mental illness or defectiveness. We, as parents, will often condemn the uninformed public, and perhaps our feelings may be somewhat justified, but we should carefully look into our own lives and find out if we have made a real attempt to discover the truth, or do we know only what has been gained by bitter experience? In doing the vast amount of research necessary to write our series of radio programs, I not only gained much information, but the freedom which this truth brought to me was amazing. I began to see the problem with some of my head and not altogether with my heart, and it takes both to achieve a sense of peace and well-being.

The fifth point is almost a corollary to the fourth: *Face your problem; don't run away from it or deny its existence.*

Parents who try to meet this problem, even in the beginning, by ignoring it are only adding to their later grief. Postponing an acceptance of mental retardation is not only a dangerous policy for the parents but can be most detrimental to the child's welfare. Irreparable damage can be done to the child's personality, and his chances for future adjustment can be immeasurably reduced by refusing to admit his limitations and expecting him to conform to a standard which is utterly impossible for him to achieve. This is not quite so likely to happen in the cases where retardation can be recognized shortly after birth, but it is a great danger in those children who look normal and do not have apparent physical symptoms which indicate retardation. If you can accept the facts and your friends know and understand the situation, there will be much less of that "now if he were my child" attitude which all parents of retarded children resent so bitterly. All of us think we know what to do (at least most of the time!) with the average child, but the child who has not developed along the so-called normal pattern must have more understanding from his neighbors and friends, as well as from his parents. Notice that we say *understanding,* not sympathy or overattention or pity—just understanding.

If all parents of retarded children would do these five things, the road to recovery would not only be a quicker one in an emotional sense, but in the end a less painful one as well.

1. Try to develop (without bitterness) immunity to the pressure of public opinion.
2. Realize and accept the fact that we are not quite normal ourselves, in an emotional sense, for a period of

time. We must make allowance for this fact, not only in our relationship with our children but with our mates, families, and friends.

3. Try to develop and maintain some absorbing interest outside your daily routine for release of emotional tension and stress. This is beneficial not only to the parents but to the child as well.

4. Inform yourself as to the actual truth about retardation.

5. Face your problem; don't try to run away from it or deny its existence.

Never believe that the accomplishment, or even the partial accomplishment, of these five things is an easy task. It will be the most difficult assignment of your life, but, as in life itself, the reward will be commensurate with the effort put forth.

Chapter Fourteen

UNDOUBTEDLY THE most difficult question which arises to face the parents of a mentally retarded child is whether that child shall be kept within the family circle or shall at some time be placed either in a private or a public institution especially planned for the care of such children. Having walked this lonely road ourselves, we feel that we have earned the right to speak.

Many persons, parents of retarded children and others, have asked me this question: "What do you think is best, to try to keep the retarded child at home or permit him to be placed in an institution?" My answer is always the same: "It altogether depends."

It depends upon the type and severity of defectiveness suffered by the child; it depends upon the personality, nature, disposition, and physical health of each of the parents; it depends upon what local facilities are available for the training of the child; it depends upon the possible effect such a child might have on other children of the family; it depends upon the ability of the family to arrange for *permanent* care within the family circle—and many other factors too numerous to name. There are so many facets to this problem that we feel it is quite impossible to say that either course is right or wrong, wise or unwise, in itself.

Many people not very familiar with the problems are tempted to generalize and say: "*This* child is an institutional case; *this* child is not." Such generalizations seem to me to be dangerous. Can we say that any particular child is an absolute institutional case, as such? We are often prone to think of the extremely low-grade, or bedridden, patient as being a typical institutional case, while the middle- or higher-grade child need not be. Although there is some good basis for this belief, yet the bed patient is in many instances far less likely to have an extremely disrupting influence on the homelife of the family than the middle- or high-grade retardate who may develop destructive tendencies and must be under constant supervision lest he unintentionally hurt either himself or another child. The child whose world is confined to one room, or to his home, never presents the problems that must be met when one is extremely active and his life must be thought of in terms of other members of the family and the public at large. On the other hand, the strain of caring for a bed patient or a wheelchair patient is a great physical one, and many times it is imperative that such a child be given institutional care for the sake of the mother's physical health. There are so many things to be considered that it seems we can hardly say a child is or is not an institutional case based on his physical and mental condition alone.

Although there was a time when most doctors recommended that all mentally defective children be institutionalized, the time has come when they are beginning to recognize that other answers to this problem must be found. To begin with, there are not enough existing institutions, either public or private, to care for even a small percentage of the mentally defective children of our nation. There is serious doubt as to whether there ever will be. It is easy enough for people to say to some distracted parent, "That child belongs in an institution," but when they come face to face with the fact that there is no room for him and perhaps will not be for years, they must realize that some rethinking will have to be done. There are a few states which have no public institutional facilities at all for the retarded child.* No matter how much he needs special care, he cannot have it because the facilities simply do not exist. Many states have colonies or training schools for the retarded, but without an exception they are overcrowded and many times understaffed with long, long waiting lists. Our own Virginia State School has had, on an average, a waiting list of more than five hundred children for a number of years. These children have been legally committed, but they can be admitted at the rate of only a few each month.

This situation will not be changed until public opinion is educated to the need of more and better equipped institutions for the mentally defective. We who are the parents of these children are among those who must help bring the public to an understanding of the need. For too many years mentally retarded children have been hidden from view and their condition ignored or denied as long as the parents could possibly do so. The subject has been one about which little has been written or said in the past. Consequently, the great need for training facilities on both a state and a local level has not been met, primarily because the need was not recognized.

---

* Although true in 1954 when written, this statement does not hold true today due to the substantial increase in all facilities for the retarded.

Some parent groups have made comprehensive surveys to ascertain the number of retarded children in their own areas. In every case, the results were astounding. In places where it was generally supposed that there were perhaps thirty or forty such children, the number has often proved to be three or four times that many. Not only parents themselves have been unaware of the number of children unable to enter the public schools because of mental limitation, but physicians, educational authorities, and others interested in the problem are amazed to find so many children being denied their natural birthright to training suited to their needs. *I am convinced that it is not indifference or lack of concern for the needs of the mentally retarded that has created this existing situation, but, primarily, a lack of information.* Once the people of our nation recognize and know the situation as it is, steps will be taken to alleviate the condition.

This will not happen until public opinion is sufficiently aroused to the need, and *public opinion will never be aroused to meet any need so long as those who are directly involved refuse to admit that the need exists.* We who are parents of these children must bend our energies toward making the needs known to the world, instead of bitterly denouncing the world because it has been so indifferent to a problem whose existence it did not recognize. This is going to take courage and stamina over and above what we believe we possess, but until we gain the courage to say to the world, "Yes, I am the parent of a mentally retarded child," we cannot expect the world to recognize and respond to the needs of this child.

Assuming that institutional care is available, under what circumstances should a child be placed there in preference to staying in his own family circle? Such a question is impossible to answer in a general way. The only thing which can be done is to point out certain factors.

To begin with, this is a problem which we believe should be decided by the parents themselves without undue pressure from outside sources. Until the parents themselves can believe that their child's welfare can best be served by institutional care, they will never be satisfied with the decision to place him away from home. This does not mean that one should not seek advice. It should be sought by all means from competent authorities, but until that advice has crystallized to the point where it is actually the thinking and feeling of the parents themselves, it surely should not be followed.

It is true that parents need to seek advice, but it cannot be emphasized too much that the people to whom they go for advice should be those who know the issues involved and are not just friends or relatives. Most of our friends or relatives cannot know what is best or wisest, in a given situation, because of their lack of experience. Also, their opinions will be so divergent that parents will only grow the more confused the more they confer. Members of one's own family will differ as to what is best; so will neighbors. It is a problem with which they are not experienced and on which they have not earned the right to speak. In our own situation we were most fortunate in having the benefit of Dr. Black's years of psychiatric work in our State School. We felt that his judgment was to be respected because of his experience. Over and above that, we knew that he had a personal interest in Stevie as well as a professional one.

There is one thing that should be taken into consideration by parents in making this decision, however: We must realize that we are so close to our problem that it is often difficult, if not actually impossible, for us to make wise judgment of the issues involved, simply because we cannot see them from every angle. Because of that, we need to have those on the outside, so to speak, point out certain facets of the problem which we either may overlook entirely or cannot see in their true perspective. If only our heads were involved instead of our hearts, we would be able to see many things that we cannot see because we are blinded by our emotions. But we must make every effort to use both in reaching a decision, and we can succeed in doing this only when we are willing to give due consideration to things which may be pointed out to us by those who have had experience in this field.

Another thing to which we need to seek a true answer is whether we are thinking in terms of the child's welfare first, and our own personal feelings second, or vice versa. Many parents will be shocked at such an idea and would no doubt deny that they were putting anything above the welfare of their child; but, being very human, we have to admit that our own stubborn pride is likely to play a very important part in decisions we make about *any* matter with which we are faced. This was one of the greatest battles that I myself had to fight. Not pride in refusing to admit that our child was retarded; we did that from the beginning. But to admit that here was a problem too big for me to cope with, too big for me to find an adequate solution for within my own family circle—this was one of the bitterest lessons I have ever had to learn. There is now no doubt in my mind that had my pride persisted to the extent that I believed myself perfectly able to meet the problem, the consequence would have been extremely detrimental, not only to our little son, but to the other three children and our marriage as well.

It is difficult, if not almost impossible, for parents to accept the fact that other people may be able to meet the needs of their child better than the parents themselves. We believe, and rightfully so, that nothing can take the place of love in the child's life, and our greatest heartache lies in believing that he will be placed in a situation where this love will not be forthcoming. To a certain extent this is true, and it would be foolish to deny it, but in this connection a factor should be pointed out which is very easily overlooked. The mentally retarded, whether in day schools or boarding institutions, develop an affection and devotion to each other that they can never quite find with the so-called normal individual. Human beings are gregarious creatures, and not anything in the world can substitute for the satisfaction of being with one's own kind.

This factor is of far more importance to the middle- or high-grade defective than to the very low grade. It would seem that we deny one of the very basic concepts of human happiness when we expect the social needs of a middle- or high-grade child to be completely met by normal people.

Strong ties of love and affection develop between these children, ties which fill that need of being loved more adequately than is sometimes possible within the child's own family circle. I have also seen nurses, doctors, and attendants care for these children with tenderness and devotion not often accorded to normal children. Of course there are cases where this is not true, but we believe them to be the exception rather than the rule. Even though institutional life cannot be considered as the ideal answer in every case, it would seem to us that a child's spirit would stand far less chance of being wounded where he is with those of his own kind than in a world where other children will forever ask: "Well, what's the *matter* with him? Why does he *act* that way?"

Many parents will hesitate to place their child in an environment where they see other children who seem to do "queer" things. Our first reaction when we see our own child against the background of other mentally retarded individuals is something like this: "But my own little child is not like these children. They have something wrong with their minds; surely he should not be placed with them because he may pick up some of their strange habits." We forget that we have seen this little child we love so much every day and almost every hour of his life—for so long, in fact, that everything he does seems perfectly normal to us —whereas to the eyes of another person some of his actions may seem strange indeed. If, as Robert Burns has so aptly said, it is difficult for us to "see oursels as others see us," it is almost impossible for us to see our little retarded children as they are seen by others.

We believe another factor to be of real significance in making the decision as to whether a child shall be placed in an institution or kept at home. It is a factor which is so obviously important that it seems almost foolish to mention it, yet it is one which is totally ignored by many parents. It is this: We sincerely believe that parents cannot come to a reasonable and fair decision one way or the other until they have thoroughly investigated all institutional facilities available to their child, either public or private. Many parents arrive at an answer to this important question without making any investigation at all. We would think it inconceivable for parents absolutely to refuse hospital care or professional treatment for a child with a serious physical disability; yet parents of mentally retarded children will refuse such care for their children when in many cases the need is much greater than that for a physically sick child. To me, it has been a never-ending source of shock and surprise to discover how many parents of retarded children know little or nothing at all about their state institutions and the service they have to offer.

Many parents have unbelievable misconceptions because they have not taken the trouble to find out the truth. It takes courage, we know. The first time my husband and I walked into a classroom of little boys in our own State Training School and they came pressing about us just to touch us and shake our hands, I thought my heart would stop beating from sheer pain at seeing so many little faces, so

many eager, lovely little boys to whom the light of intellect
had been denied in some degree. Their joy at having com-
pany was unbounded; we have since learned that when many
of them are brought to the school, that is the end of their
contact with their families and the outside world. The
teacher showed us some of their handwork and explained
some of her teaching methods. I left the room with tears
streaming down my face. The thought that someday my own
little son might possibly be among their number was more
than I could bear. We were deeply grateful to my sister for
helping us in the initial stage of our investigation about
institutional life. Her experience in working with mental
defectives in another state proved helpful to us in knowing
what to expect from our own state institution.

Although we have made no attempt to answer yes
or no to the question of institutionalization on an individual
basis, here are some questions we should surely ask ourselves in relation to this problem:

Is my child reasonably happy? Can we truly say that
he is getting satisfaction from living commensurate with
his ability to do so?

Is his presence in our home causing tensions that may
become serious enough to endanger our marriage relationship? Are we thinking of the welfare of this child over
and above our own feeling in the matter?

What effect is the presence of a retarded child having
on the other children of the family? (This is a question
which it is almost impossible for us to answer without
benefit of observations from one on the outside of the

family; and these observations should be sought even though they may really hurt. To this day I am thankful for a friend who had the courage to point out certain reactions in my older children to which I was totally blind.)

Is the presence of a retarded child in the home demanding so much time and attention from us as parents that the needs of other children in the family are being neglected? (This should not be limited to physical needs but should include emotional and spiritual ones as well.)

Can our children invite their friends into our home freely (and *do* they) without fear of being embarrassed by their little retarded brother or sister?

Is there any local training available for my child?

These are only a few of the many questions we need to ask ourselves in trying to follow the right course for our own particular situation. There are dozens of others, but the biggest problem lies not in the number of questions but in being able to answer them honestly. There is no one in all the world with whom it is so hard to be completely honest as one's own self. Most of us have the inborn capacity for rationalizing with ourselves until we believe not the truth but what we want to believe. And in many cases, the more intellectual we are the greater danger there is in our rationalization.

If the decision is made to place a child in an institution, public or private, there is one point which, I believe, cannot be overemphasized. It is this: *Keep in touch with your child.* For many years the idea of "putting a child away" and forgetting about him has been advanced to parents. It just so happened when God made parents he did not include a very good "forgetter" as far as their children are concerned. *We aren't made to forget; we are made to remember.* And no matter what it costs us in terms of pride, of time, or of anything else that may be named, we need to remember for the sake of the child as well as for our own emotional good. In cases where a child is of such low grade that he does not know his parents from other persons, the need for seeing him is somewhat lessened; but even in these cases, parents need to go occasionally to see that the child is being well cared for just for their own peace of mind. Parents should know that the first few visits to a child after he has been placed in an institution will be most difficult to face. For a while the emotional shock of going is such that one may well wonder if he can continue to face it; but as time goes on and the child begins to become adjusted to the routine of institutional life, the visits become less painful for child and parents alike.

We should at all times remember that the wishes of the authorities should be respected in regard to visiting patients, because they know so well what damage may be caused by an ill-timed or overemotional visit from the child's parents. Parents should also understand that every child is different and that whereas one child may have visitors shortly after being admitted without serious emotional upheaval, another child may be much better off if he does not see his parents very soon. Here, again, we must respect the judgment of those who work with the children rather than follow our own personal wishes. For those parents who cannot see their children often because of distance, letters and cards provide a happy medium of contact. A brightly colored card with a stick of gum, or a dime, taped to it will bring joy out of all proportion to the small amount of time it takes to prepare it for mailing. Nearly every state institution has a canteen to which patients may go for small needs. These little excursions with their nickels and dimes provide a great satisfaction in a somewhat routine life.

After visiting our own little son a number of times, we now gain much joy in bringing some small amount of love to the other little boys on his ward, many of whom greet us with a great deal of enthusiasm. One of the things about retarded children which has never ceased to impress me is their gratitude for even the smallest attention. When I think of many normal children whose wants are never satisfied and who demand more and more from their parents, yet appreciate what they have less and less, I cannot help but think of the joy which one small bit of gum and a pat on the head bring to many of these little "forgotten children." I hope to live long enough to see the day when all states will have not one but several state homes located within driving distance of many parents so that the parents can help provide more of the personal love and attention these little children need.

Parents who try to forget they have a retarded child by pouring their energies into other causes will never find quite the same healing that can come by trying to bring happiness to these most innocent of God's little children.

They should be encouraged to remember not only their own child but also the hundreds of others who have been forsaken by their families in the belief that it was a terrible disgrace to admit to the world that they were the parents of a retarded child.

The healing which comes to our wounded spirits from this open admission and service to other children is a painful one, particularly at first, but as time goes on we begin to find an unbelievable happiness in bringing a small degree of joy and light where, before, there was only despondency and darkness.

Any parent who has read this chapter with the belief that it will provide the answer to his or her problem, may come to the close of it very much disappointed. We do not aim to influence anyone's thinking in one direction or another; these words are written only in the hope that those who read them will seek diligently for the truth, to see their problem from every angle, and also to encourage one never to abandon or try to forget a child in any sense. I only hope that I have not failed completely in trying to bring some light to this darkest of all the many problems we have to face.

Chapter Fifteen

ALL OVER the country, like mushrooms suddenly bursting through the ground on a warm spring morning, parent groups are springing into action really to do something about the problems posed by their mentally crippled children. Some of these parent groups have been in existence for a number of years, but it has been only within a brief number of years that efforts are being coordinated on a national scale. The national organization, known as the National Association for Retarded Children, embraces most of the state and local groups working in the interest of the mentally retarded. It is to be sincerely hoped that in the near future all such local and state groups will become actively affiliated with the NARC. Our problem is bigger than the individual child, broader than the community, larger than our states, and even greater than our nation; it is in truth a worldwide one, and all our efforts must be coordinated into creating a better world, not for "my child" alone, but for all such children.

Those of us who are benefactors should never lose sight of the debt of gratitude we owe to those loyal, farseeing, and hard working individuals who were pioneers in this movement. It was our good fortune to learn to know one of these pioneers in the person of Mr. Woodhull Hay. Mr. and Mrs. Hay and their retarded daughter, Barbara, spent two weeks near our farm taking a much-needed vacation just three weeks prior to Mr. Hay's untimely death. Each day Barbara came to stay with me while her mother and father read, rested, shopped, and played golf. Every day when they came to bring Barbara in the morning and to get her in the afternoon we had long talks—about many things, because, indeed, Mr. Hay was one of the most delightful conversationalists it has been my privilege to know; but regardless of where we started or what we talked about, inevitably we ended on the thing closest to our hearts, our retarded children. Mr. Hay had attended the meeting of the national association in California just prior to coming to Virginia, and he was filled with enthusiasm and plans for the future of the NARC, many of which he shared with us. Preparation of the manuscript for this book came as a direct result of one of Mr. Hay's suggestions to us as to ways in which we could best serve this cause. It was with a real sense of personal loss that we heard of his death within a few weeks of his having been with us. Even though this was a terrific blow to the newborn NARC, we knew that there would be someone whom he had inspired sufficiently to step in and carry on the work which he had so ably helped to begin.

For the benefit of those who may not know, perhaps it would be good to point out briefly some of the things which these parent groups have already accomplished. One of the most tangible results has been the numerous local training classes which have been set up through the organized efforts of parents. In most instances there was absolutely no provision for training retarded children on a local level so that the child could remain in his own home. Today, primarily because of local parent associations, this situation has been remedied in many cities and towns.

Much state legislation in behalf of the mentally retarded has been passed because the parents themselves have brought the legislators to an awareness of the needs. State training schools and colonies for the defective have benefited everywhere because of the interest of parent associations. Special equipment, toys, entertainment—the list of things done for those who are in our institutions is a long and encouraging one. A broad, general program for educating the public to the needs of, and acceptance of these children is under way by magazine articles, books, radio, and television. Everywhere people are being made aware of the fact that these children exist and that their needs must be met just the same as those of all God's other children.

I am convinced that the dilemma in which we find ourselves today in regard to a lack of institutional facilities exists not because of a cruel and misunderstanding public, but only because the public has not been aware that so many of these children needed their help. Why is this true? Because many parents have refused to admit that their child was different and *needed* special care. Why or how can I as a parent condemn the public for the fact that no special training provisions are made for my child if I have refused to admit that he needed special provision because of mental limitation? Perhaps these are searching words, but let us not become bitter toward others for a situation which has developed partly because of our own pride.

Through the NARC, efforts are being coordinated in

setting up more clinics for the examination of retarded children. There is also a research program in progress under the guidance of the NARC. We believe that implementing research into the causes of mental retardation is one of the most vital fields in which our national organization can serve.

Perhaps one of the most valuable aspects of this parent movement is an intangible one—the therapeutic value which working for the good of these children brings to the individual parents. When we begin working together to improve conditions not only for our own child, but all others as well, a real healing begins to take place, and we begin to believe that life once again has meaning and purpose.

It is interesting to note that in no other area of life are people with such diversified interests, tastes, and backgrounds likely to be brought together to work for a common cause. Our civilization is so arranged that most of our interests and our work are connected with people of like interests and work. Mental defectiveness recognizes no race, creed, or social standing; hence, in these organizations we have members of every race and creed, every stratum of society, every profession, every grade of economic level working together for one common purpose—that of changing the world which our retarded children now know for a better one.

Because of these vast differences, because of the difference in the needs of our individual children, and simply because people are *people,* each of us as individuals will have to grow and grow and grow some more in a spiritual sense so that our efforts will be unified and purposeful. All of us need to recognize that we feel so intensely about this entire problem that we may not always be as patient and understanding with one another as we should be in trying to reach our common objective. We must not let our enthusiasm for our own ideas and opinions blind us to the fact that others may have ideas and opinions just as valuable as our own, even though they do not coincide precisely with ours. Every parent, no matter how limited he may be in some respects, can do something for the alleviation of this problem. For those who may have been blessed with some specific ability or training the task may be a very large and difficult one, but for *every* parent there is a job to be done. I have been struck forcibly in our own local association with the willingness with which most parents will respond to any work they feel they can do. Our enthusiasm is great because our need is so great.

The work we are doing today will not bring big rewards immediately, and many parents will become greatly discouraged when miracles are not wrought overnight. Those of us in the orchard business come to think not in terms of weeks, or months, or even years, but in terms of generations. We need to develop this same farseeing view in relation to improving conditions for our retarded children. Our aims will not all be accomplished easily; neither will they be accomplished quickly. It will take years of patient, sacrificial effort. But if in future generations *life's road for the retarded has become paved with understanding and landscaped with affection and opportunity,* who will there be to say our labor has been in vain? We are laying the foundation for that road today. It is to be hoped that we will seek the guidance of an all-wise Father that this foundation may be laid with the wisdom which will make such a road not only a highway of happiness for future retarded children, but will, in itself, be an honor to his great and holy name. Such a highway cannot help but lead *out of darkness, into light.*

EPILOGUE

WRITTEN IN 1966, ten years after publication of
the original edition of *This Is Stevie's Story*.

Chapter Sixteen

When Stevie was admitted to the Lynchburg Training School and Hospital in February, 1952, as a frightened, speechless, and withdrawn little retarded boy of seven, we believed that it would be for life. Fourteen years have now elapsed, and this year he will return to live in our home as a happy, well-adjusted young retarded adult, partially self-supporting and secure in the knowledge that he is a loved and respected member of his family, his community, and indeed of society at large.

It is not by mere chance that this is so. Three factors have contributed to make the happy ending of his story possible: first, the dozens of professional people down through the years who have worked patiently and persistently to help Stevie develop and use his limited mental faculties to the maximum; second, the growth and understanding on our part as his parents in learning how to cope with and adjust to the multiplicity of problems that confront families with a retarded member; and third, the dedicated efforts of thousands of laymen and professionals working through the local and state groups and the National Association for Retarded Children to bring about a social revolution that is helping to create a new world for the mentally retarded—a world in which they can eventually live with the same privileges and dignity accorded to all other citizens. About fifteen years ago the parent of a mentally retarded child stood before the members of the legislature in his state and declared prophetically: "There may be some doubt as to how much we can change our children for the world's sake, but there is no doubt that we have to change the world for our children's sake." And it is against this exciting and hopeful background of a changing world that our Stevie's story is now destined for a much happier conclusion than we would have dared dream possible fourteen years ago.

The first four years of Stevie's life in residential care produced very little change in his overall development. Although he did become less hyperactive and destructive, we saw little improvement in his ability to communicate or to relate to those around him. But at the age of eleven he had the good fortune to come into the care of a speech therapist, Mrs. Johnson, who was to play a large part in liberating him from the bondage of loneliness, of frustration, and many of the other psychological chains that literally bind many of the mentally retarded within themselves. Armed with a warm-hearted love for children plus her hard-won know-how as a speech therapist, she was able to do for Stevie what no other individual up to this point had been successful in doing.

This is in no way to infer that she was the only person who had helped him. Down through the years there had been a succession of teachers, psychologists, attendants, and others who had done for him what they could, and to each of them we shall ever be grateful; but it was the speech therapist who finally found the key to unlock the seemingly impenetrable wall of loneliness behind which Stevie seemed to take refuge. After two years under her careful and painstaking tutelage he finally began to relate not only to her but to his family and other people around him. With his newly found ability to communicate, many of his peculiar mannerisms and symptoms of unhappiness and loneliness began very slowly to disappear.

Our satisfaction in his progress, however, was made less joyful by the fact that it brought us face to face with one of the most difficult decisions of our lives. For two years he had made such unusual progress that Mrs. Johnson came to the conclusion that Stevie's problem of retardation was further complicated by a condition known as aphasia, a type of brain damage which affects the part of the brain that functions in speech development. Much of the speech therapy technique which had proved so successful with him had been used with many aphasic children, and his unusual response led her logically to believe that a more intensive emphasis on therapy for aphasia would definitely be to his benefit. With his best interest at heart Mrs. Johnson felt that we should seriously consider the possibility of taking him out of our state Training School for the retarded and sending him to a school for aphasic children in another state.

She felt, and quite sincerely I am sure, that this might be our final and last opportunity to do much for Stevie, as he was rapidly approaching puberty and any intensive training would probably have its greatest effect at this time.

There are no words to describe the days and weeks of agonizing indecision through which we passed that year. The problem of finance was very real because the school in question was an extremely expensive one, and we had been frankly advised that we should think in terms of not less than four to six years of treatment. Although we did not have the money available, we believed that we could borrow it. We realized, however, that this might jeopardize our ability to send the other three children to college in future years.

There was another factor, too, which added to our confusion. At the time Stevie entered the Training School at the age of seven a young psychiatrist there had suggested to us that he showed more symptoms of childhood autism (a severe form of mental illness in children) than of mental retardation. Several other professional people had suggested this possibility also, and I myself recognized that many of the symptoms he exhibited were distinctly characteristic of the autistic child. So what should we do? We had long ago come to terms with the fact that he was mentally retarded and that for the good of our family as well as for Stevie himself we must place him in residential care. But now we were faced with a new series of questions. Was he an autistic child rather than a mentally retarded one? If so, had we wasted years of valuable time by not having him under appropriate treatment for autism? Was his basic problem one of aphasia, as recent evidence appeared to indicate, or was it primarily mental retardation? (Although Mrs. Johnson did not discount the possibility of mental retardation, her suggestion that he be placed in the school for aphasic children did cause us as parents to wonder if this might be the primary problem. Like many other parents, we were to discover later that in the field of mental retardation a little learning was most truly a dangerous thing!) Was it right to risk our family's financial future in order to provide Stevie with specialized training that might have the possibility of making him a fully self-sustaining member of society? If the primary problem was not mental retardation, would leaving him at the Training School with 2,500 other retardates be to his detriment? Should we bring him home and try to do what we could for him? These and many other questions haunted us, and our faith was somewhat shaken in our own ability to make decisions and judgments that were for the best of all concerned. Too, we had become a trifle cynical and not a little bit confused over some of the professional advice we had received over a period of years.

Just about the time we reached twin peaks of desperation and indecision a new superintendent, Dr. Benedict Nagler, came to the Training School. Not being familiar with our total problem, Dr. Nagler nevertheless recognized our need for immediate help, and he made arrangements for Stevie to be seen at one of the country's foremost medical centers and for us to talk with one of the staff consultants there, Dr. Leo Kanner, a highly respected child psychiatrist known throughout the world for his writing and teaching in the fields of both mental illness and mental retardation in children. With his characteristic thoroughness for detail and efficiency in the use of time, Dr. Nagler sent Dr. Kanner all Stevie's medical records as well as a copy of *This Is Stevie's Story* (which had been published two years before) in order that he might be somewhat familiar with the background of his case and with our family situation. Thus it was that on a bleak March morning in 1958 Max and I arrived with Stevie at the children's clinic at Johns Hopkins to seek help in making the decisions which we knew would be vital not only to his welfare but to that of our entire family.

"Just why, may I ask, have you come here to see me?"

It was Dr. Kanner speaking, and the question startled both of us into the realization that he must indeed really wonder why we were there, since we had so obviously long ago accepted the fact that Stevie was mentally retarded and had been satisfied with our decision made almost seven years before to place him in residential care.

"I suppose the real reason we're here is that we now have a decision to make about Stevie that we just can't make without help," replied Max.

"And to be quite frank, we're here partly because we've become so completely confused by conflicting professional opinions we've heard over a period of years that we just don't know what to believe," I blurted out somewhat defensively.

Dr. Kanner took several long, relaxed puffs on his ever-present long black cigar. "What do you mean by that, Mrs.

Murray?" He asked the question quite honestly, but even at the time I had a feeling he already knew the answer!

I assured him that for the most part our experiences with professionals had been most helpful and satisfactory but that even honest differences of opinion and judgment could be most upsetting to parents of retarded children, to say nothing of the damage done by those who were thoughtless and sometimes apparently heartless in their observations. Almost against my own will I found myself spilling out in a torrent of words several of my own experiences which had shaken me to the extent that I was beginning to be convinced that my own ineptness and lack of common sense were completely responsible for Stevie's condition.

There was the eye, ear, nose, and throat specialist, for instance, who had asserted to me quite flatly that "there's nothing in the world wrong with your little boy's mind, but you will surely make it so if you go around talking about the fact so freely. Just go home and take care of this boy and quit running all over the country trying to make an imaginary mental problem when there is none there." This choice bit of "professional advice" had come to me only four months after we had first been told of Stevie's condition, while I was still in a state of complete emotional shock. Although he had been seen several times by two psychiatrists, had gone through a series of psychological and hearing tests, had been observed at length by a woman with thirty years of experience in teaching the mentally retarded, all of whom agreed there was little if any doubt that he was mentally retarded, yet here was a reputable, highly respected specialist making this flat assertion to me the first time he saw Stevie to make a brief and cursory examination of his tonsils and adenoids! His judgment was made simply because I had indicated to the nurse taking Stevie's medical record that they might have to make some allowance for him during their examination because he did not talk and might not respond fully to their directions, since his mental development had not been normal.

There had been other times: the rigid social worker, for instance, who was quite confident in her judgment that our only problem was one of complete mismanagement and poor guidance on my part and that a few sound spankings and a little "proper discipline" would correct any problems we were having, including Stevie's inability to talk. Shortly before talking with her, we had been advised by an equally astute professional in the field of child care, a mother of eight and grandmother of eighteen, that physical punishment should be used sparingly in Stevie's case, if at all. And so it went.

"Now how, Dr. Kanner, how in the name of common sense are parents supposed to sift the wheat from the chaff in all the advice they receive, not only from professional people but from friends and relatives as well?" I asked with intensity.

A few more thoughtful puffs on his cigar—and soon both Max and I were as relaxed as the good doctor himself. Someone has wisely observed that "one gets it off one's chest by getting it on one's tongue." Dr. Kanner, with his knowledge accumulated through many years of study and experience, recognized our need for this kind of therapy. He gave us an opportunity to get a good many things off our chests, an accumulation of problems—some real, some imaginary. Then with the wisdom born from years of experience as well as a genuine caring for all humankind, he began the process of helping to restore and reinforce our confidence in making our own decisions and judgments. He pointed out the disadvantage which had been ours because Stevie had been seen piecemeal, so to speak, instead of in a diagnostic clinic where his problem could be studied and evaluated by a team of specialists as a whole rather than in its specific parts with each professional discipline rendering an individual opinion without the overall judgment of a team. In careful and simple language that we could fully comprehend (no smoke screen of technical jargon behind which many an insecure, self-styled expert tends to hide), Dr. Kanner explained the fact that professional misjudgments about mental retardation were often reached because a specialist in a certain field saw in the child only that particular part of the problem with which he or she was most familiar instead of the total picture. He explained that in making an accurate diagnosis of mental retardation one must be somewhat familiar with the entire spectrum of the problem and not just with one or two facets, as was often the case when one had practiced for only a short while within a specific professional discipline. "This, I suspect, may be what has happened with the apparently very good speech therapist who has been working with your little son. She sees only that one part of his problem which relates to a type of brain damage that interferes with speech development. Since he is responding so favorably to her corrective training in speech therapy, it would be quite easy to conclude that this is his major problem instead of mental retardation."

Dr. Kanner went on to explain many other things which helped us to take a more mature and discerning look at our own reactions so as to make us more understanding of and less disturbed by what might later prove to be professional misjudgments. Dr. Kanner himself was the child psychiatrist who had brought to light some fifteen years before the condition of mental illness in children known as autism. He had done a considerable amount of writing and lecturing concerning this one facet of mental illness. He told us that he had had literally thousands of children, including our Stevie, referred to him by physicians and others throughout the world who were fairly certain that the children they were sending were suffering from this condition. Out of the thousands he had seen, Dr. Kanner asserted that he had found only a very, very small percent who were truly autistic. The vast majority were like Stevie—they were basically mentally retarded children even though they had many symptoms of autism present at one period or another in their early development. According to Dr. Kanner, a child in whom these symptoms were quite pronounced could—and quite frequently did—receive an incorrect diagnosis in the hands of even very good professionals whose experience with both mental illness and retardation had been limited. He helped us to see that in matters involving the development of the intellect there was yet much to be learned and that many conscientious and able professionals could and did err in their judgment.

So well did Dr. Kanner advise us that day that I could be mildly amused about an experience I had within the past year, whereas had such a thing happened fifteen years ago, I probably would have gone into a complete emotional tailspin. At a small social event recently I was engaged in conversation with an individual widely known and respected in the field of mental retardation. He was gracious enough to ask me a few questions about Stevie, and on the basis of the answers I gave him concerning some of the things he could now do, he made the positive statement that in his opinion Stevie was not mentally retarded at all because if he were he simply would be incapable of doing these things. He had never seen Stevie, had seen none of his medical records, had only met me minutes before, knew absolutely nothing concerning the professional judgment that had been rendered about Stevie down through the years, and yet this expert was ready to make the flat statement that everybody had been incorrect in diagnosis! And this based merely on Steve's present achievements, which though quite wonderful to us are indeed very, very limited. Upon hearing his cocksure assertion, I could only be thankful to the core that I had long ago outgrown the naïve belief that every opinion rendered by a recognized authority was sacrosanct. I shuddered, however, to think what effect an individual of his professional stature might possibly have on a set of new parents who were grasping at every straw in hopes of finding someone who would declare their child not mentally retarded. Such false hope held out to the parents of retarded children does far more damage than the keen, sharp cut which is made by the professional person who has the wisdom and the courage to make them face the truth, cold and stark as it may be.

We left Johns Hopkins after two days of testing for Stevie and conferences for us. Dr. Kanner had given us much constructive help and advice, but above that he had given us the most priceless gift of all—a restoration of faith in ourselves and confidence in our ability to make the necessary decisions for Stevie's best welfare in the coming years. At the close of our final interview with him we rose to leave, and as he shook hands with us warmly he gave us these parting words: "No, your little son is not an autistic child. Neither is his primary problem one of aphasia, although he does have some pronounced symptoms of both these conditions. What you have is a sweet little mentally retarded boy. You had adjusted to that fact long ago. Now go back home and continue to do for Stevie just what you have done in the past. Give him plenty of love and all the opportunity for training you can reasonably afford without denying opportunities to your other three children, and make each decision about his care in the years to come on the basis of your best knowledge and the current circumstances."

Our own experience and that of hundreds of parents with whom I have talked over the past fifteen years leads me to believe that one of the greatest problems with which we have to cope is that of the conflicting professional opinions to which we will inevitably be exposed over a period of years. It is my opinion that most professional people have no conception of the amount of psychological havoc that is wrought in the minds of parents of a mentally retarded child when they are exposed to incompatible ideas concerning their child's diagnosis, prognosis, or treatment programs. We as parents are particularly vulnerable during the early years of the child's life because we come to professionals innocently believing that each one is an avowed expert in his or her own particular field. But when one so-believed expert asserts without qualification that "this is the problem and this is the solution," and another equally recognized authority within the same discipline begs to disagree (this happens more often than one would believe!), then the parent is faced with having to make a choice as to which declaration is right or wrong. Further consultation may only add to the confusion, and the problems are compounded when authorities of another discipline are brought into the picture and in turn express ideas that are quite contrary to those already expressed. Fortunately the picture is quite different today from what it was when Stevie was young. Then there were no diagnostic clinics— no place to turn for a comprehensive picture of the problem. Because of the efforts of the associations for retarded children, most states now have diagnostic clinics within reach of most parents, and the child does not need to be seen piecemeal fashion as was true in days gone by. This in itself will do much to alleviate the problems created for parents by ill-advised, ill-timed, and inept expressions of professional opinion.

Maturity is required on the part of both parents and professional people if the welfare of the retardate is to be served to the best advantage. For the parent this demands that we study and make appropriate use of all information currently available to us. It also demands that we make an effort to develop the kind of self-knowledge and self-understanding that enables us to feel reasonably secure in the numerous decisions which must be made down through the years—decisions which will not only relate to the retarded person alone but which will affect the welfare of the entire family. Maturity on the part of the professional is indicated by the fact that he or she is ever open to new knowledge, new insight. We believe, too, that the truly mature person within any discipline dealing in mental retardation will remain ever cognizant of his or her limitation in dealing with the many unknown factors relating to the development of the human intellectual capacity. Above all, true maturity in the professional person requires that his primary goal in life be to serve those who so desperately need his help and not merely to promote his own professional reputation or defensively nourish an ego that may at times be challenged by those who differ with him.

Chapter Seventeen

STEVIE'S YEARS between twelve and twenty at the Training School were filled with slow but gradual progress. Along with his rapidly increasing physical stature we felt he should have the dignity of a name that did not sound like a little boy, so we, along with his schoolmates and others, began addressing him as Stephen or Steve. How much difference this made to him we were really never sure, but at least he was accorded the signs of usual respect of growing into manhood, and for the retarded we feel this is of particular importance. With his newly discovered and slowly developing ability to communicate more freely, his entire personality began to blossom. He came home regularly for many weekend visits and for all holidays and an extended vacation each summer. We took him on numerous trips with the family, and these he enjoyed to the fullest.

The summer Steve was thirteen our oldest daughter was to be married in a church wedding. Both her Daddy and I had some reservations about whether we should bring Steve home for the wedding. This was to be Anne and Sam's day, and we certainly wanted to be sure that nothing would mar the joy of the occasion for them. We believed, though, that Steve would enjoy the happy event even though he might not fully understand what it was all about. In a somewhat roundabout fashion and with an attempt at casualness I mentioned our concern to Anne just to see what her reaction

would be. She responded in her usual forthright manner:
"Why of course we'll have Steve home for our wedding,
Mother. I hadn't even thought of anything else. After all,
he's part of our *family*, isn't he?" It was as simple as that,
no beating about the bush, no flimsy excuses, no worry over
whether Steve might do some bizarre thing that could prove
embarrassing. This was an important family occasion, and
Steve was a part of our family, so he would be there. The
chaplain at the Training School, Mrs. Caressa Morgan, who
had long since become a warm personal friend of mine,
brought Steve to the wedding, and the sight of his shining
brown eyes when Anne walked down the aisle in her wedding
gown brought an extra shine to some other eyes than my
own, and all of it wasn't due to the solemnity of the moment,
either.

Four years later Max's parents celebrated their golden
wedding anniversary, and I can see Steve yet, a gangling
six-foot-four seventeen-year-old bending over the guest book,
printing his name in large block letters with the painstaking
effort that was so characteristic of him. Several years later
he was to announce with great pride to his teachers and
schoolmates that he was going home to his big brother's wedding, and this gave us all a bit of a chuckle because by now
Steve had outgrown Andy by several inches. Seeing him at
Andy's wedding, so happy, so completely accepted by all
around him, I could only recall with a lump in my throat
the day I had held Andy on my knee to explain why Steve
must go away from us to live and Andy's tearful protest

that Steve couldn't go "because Mother, he's part of our *family*."

Our two older children's marriages to two fine young people who fully accept and love Steve for what he is brings me to discuss one more problem which looms large and foreboding in the minds of all parents of mentally retarded children. I know it is so because it was true in our own situation, and I have talked with dozens of parents who have agreed that this is one of their more serious concerns in the initial stages of their adjustment to life with a retarded person as a member of the family. When we first learned of Steve's condition, I recall to this day the icy fear which gripped my heart that this might very well affect the possibility of our other three children entering into warm and satisfying marriages. I recalled with much misgiving the emphasis that had been brought to bear throughout my own younger years concerning the matter of "good blood lines" and the desirability of marriage into family lines that contained no "hereditary taints." When I looked at our own small, helpless son and realized that his condition might well be a contributing factor toward future sorrow for our other three children, my heart broke all over again, not once but many times. Perhaps our passionate desire for the future welfare and happiness of our other three children contributed to our strong motivation to help make the truth about mental retardation known to the world. I remember with sadness a conversation with a set of parents who had come to see me from a distant town to talk about placing their own little retarded son in residential care. They were also the parents of two young girls, one

rapidly approaching her teens, and it was primarily for her
sake they planned to take this step. "You see, Mrs. Murray,
we just can't afford to let Billy's condition stand in the way
of Marcia's chance for a normal social life and proper marriage. We plan to move to another city to live where we are
not known, and this will afford our daughters their rightful
opportunity to good marriages," the father explained.

"But what will happen," I injected candidly, "what will
happen when someday your Marcia is ready for marriage?
You surely won't permit her to marry someone without his
knowing about Billy, will you?"

"Well, I suppose we will just have to worry about that
when the time comes," the mother replied with hopeless sadness. I tried to help them see that marriage for their daughters, no matter how promising, would begin on terribly shaky
ground if based on any falsehood, and especially on any matter so serious as this. I never saw the parents again and never
knew their final decision, but I hope the new knowledge
about mental retardation which has been made public in the
intervening years may have enabled their daughters to make
happy marriages based on the solid foundation of scientific
fact and open frankness rather than on folklore and faulty
attempts at covering up the existence of the sweet, pathetic
little boy whom they were consigning to the role of a family
skeleton. Most of all, I fervently hoped that their delightful
and winsome little Mongoloid Billy had not been relegated
to that host of hopeless, hollow-eyed, waiting children I had
seen in residential centers for the retarded throughout the

nation. Forever and always they were waiting—waiting for
parents who never came, waiting for the love of brothers and
sisters who had been led to believe it was the part of ex-
pediency to deny their existence. Such false reasoning as
this only compounds the sorrow of families with a retarded
member, and all of them suffer, but the sorrow of the retardate who sadly and hopelessly waits is the most poignant
of all.

I recall another conversation with an internationally known
sports figure whose name was a household word for years in
all families with young boys. He knew about Steve, and I
was the first outside person with whom he had ever dis-
cussed openly and frankly the fact that he had been the
brother of a mentally retarded girl. He was intensely interested in all that I could tell him about the beginning of
the National Association for Retarded Children. At the conclusion of our two-hour discussion he made this comment:
"Had I known some of the things you have told me here
tonight, it may have made a difference in our lives. My wife
and I literally went through hell during the time we were
having our family for fear we would produce a retarded child
like my sister. Now we learn too late that it wasn't necessary."

Yes, it was too late for them, too late for many of us and
for our retarded children as well as for their brothers and
sisters. But it is not too late for the millions of the future
who will marry and produce families. For the sake of these,
added truth about mental retardation must be discovered
through continued research into the genetic causes for men-

tal retardation. When additional scientific research has firmly established more of the basic facts concerning the genetic
causes of mental retardation, it will then be possible to provide
prospective parents with genetic counseling which may alleviate some of their deep concerns about giving birth to a
retarded child.

The summer of 1963 was a momentous one for our entire
family. For the first time in eleven years since Stevie had
gone to the Training School all the children were home with
us for the summer. Anne's husband, Sam, who was em-
ployed by the government, had been sent to Berlin on a two-
year assignment in May, and Anne came to spend the summer
with us to await the birth of their first child before joining
him. It was a full and exciting three months for all of us.
Elaine's beloved horse Lady gave birth to her first colt and
created so much excitement that Anne was to declare somewhat wanly she thought having her own baby would be a
kind of anticlimax! Andy soon acquired his charming and
talented bride, Teresa, and shortly after their return Anne's
baby, our first grandchild, Mary Willard, was born. Steve
was quite proud of his new status of being an uncle, and not
to be outdone by all the acquisitions of the other three children he got a broken foot! The broken foot was not without
its benefits, however. All the extra attention he received at
home and at the summer camp for the retarded tended to
give Steve's ego a real boost, and we think he began to be
convinced that summer that he was just as important as
everybody else and that with a little bit of extra effort he

could do a lot of unexpected things. Things like learning to swim, for instance. And holding Anne's new baby while she had her apple juice or water. He was most gentle and tender with the baby and seemed to get a very special kind of pleasure out of holding her while he played with her dainty fingers and toes. His leg and foot were in a cast from late June until August, and during that time he sat every day by our small swimming pool or at the pool at camp and watched the other children swim. On the very day the cast was removed from his leg he got into the pool and swam from one side to the other just as though he had been swimming all his life.

Yes, the passing years brought their small triumphs and accomplishments for Steve. There was the night, for instance, when he had gone bowling with Elaine's Sunday school class on a weekend visit home from the Training School. It was his very first trip to a bowling alley. Someone handed him the ball when his turn came and told him to knock the pins down. He walked over and let the ball go—to make the only strike of the evening! Not only Elaine but all the others were quite surprised and noisily excited over his apparent skill, while Steve appeared to be only mildly interested in what had happened. After all, they had told him to knock down the pins, hadn't they? And he had just simply done what they told him to. What in the world was all the excitement about?

The passing years not only brought their small accomplishments—they brought a few tears, too, tears for what might have been but we knew would never be. There was the night I went alone to the baccalaureate service for the local high school graduating class. As the graduates marched in to the stately strains of "Pomp and Circumstance," the girls so young and lovely, the fellows with their typically studied air of nonchalance crossed with solemnity, all at once like the proverbial bolt from the blue it struck me that this was Steve's class, these were the boys and girls born the year he was, the group with which he should have been sharing all the joys and sorrows of growing up and graduating. For one fleeting moment I was blinded by the stinging and poignant tears that came to remind me of what might have been. Such moments do not come quite so often now, but they do come, and I'm sure they always will. Memories brought back by a tune he loved as a small baby, the hurt look that still crosses his handsome face when he cannot comprehend what seems so obvious to all about him—these are the memories that come to bless and burn as we move through life. Like all such parents, however, I simply add the pearls of these poignant moments to an ever-growing string of such memories, and as I sat there in the auditorium during the service of the evening I was thankful for the darkness that permitted me to keep my sorrow for my own. As I listened to the minister talk to the graduating class about their future contribution to society, I was struck anew with the fact that Steve and all the millions like him could not hope to make such a contribution, would in fact probably be an economic and social burden to society down through the years through no fault of their own.

And yet, who is there to say that they do not contribute in their own unique way? During the past fifteen years I have worked with the Association for Retarded Children on a local, state, and national level, holding numerous offices and spending many days and weeks in committee work with parents as well as with professional people. It has been my privilege to have talked with thousands of parents, and one of the favorite themes that permeate our conversation is how much our children have meant to us. This thought runs like a bright golden thread through the dark tapestry of our sorrow. We learn so much from our children because retarded people are wonderful teachers if we are not too proud to learn from them, and the grief of parents leaves little room for pride. We learn so much in patience, in humility, in gratitude for other blessings we had accepted before as a matter of course, so much in tolerance, so much in faith—believing where we cannot see—so much in compassion for our fellowman, and yes, even so much in wisdom about the eternal values of life because deep agony of spirit is the one thing which can turn us from the superficialities of life to the things that really matter. We also gain much in developing a strange kind of courage which enables us to face life without cringing, because in one sense we have borne the ultimate that life has to offer in sorrow and pain. Where in this vast, wide world could we go to learn such lessons as these—lessons dealing with the real meaning of life? Where else could we ever hope to learn so much from those who know so little?

Although Steve was unable to graduate from high school, or even from elementary school for that matter, other things were happening to him that indicated progress. Under the careful tutelage of a patient home economics teacher at the Training School he was learning to cook. His first biscuits, cookies, and muffins made at home were given more praise than would have been accorded the cuisine of a French chef! We found that with careful explanation he could do many small helpful jobs about the house and farm, and most of them he performed with real pride. It was during this period that we began to think seriously about the possibility of having him come home to live with us after he had had the benefit of all they could do for him at the Training School. He had spent the summers with us for the past six years, and each passing year we saw him grow a little more sure of himself, more eager to contribute in any way he could to the total family welfare.

It was during this period, too, that I had absorbed much of the philosophy of Dr. Gunnar Dybwad, who at that time was serving as the Executive Director of our National Association for Retarded Children. Dr. Dybwad had always stoutly maintained that the mentally retarded could do far more than had ever been expected from them if they had the chance for good training and were given the opportunity to work in an environment suited to their needs. Speaking before a meeting of the American Public Health Association in San Francisco, November 3, 1960, Dr. Dybwad declared in his typically vehement fashion: "In general the observation can be made that in the past we concentrated too much on developing classifications which denoted our preconceived notions of the retardate's limitations and then proceeded to restrict his program and his opportunity to grow in accordance with our notions! Clinical evidence clearly demonstrates two factors: An intelligence test, such as the Stanford-Binet, is not by itself an adequate measuring device of a retarded individual's potentiality. Furthermore, research in Europe and this country shows that severely as well as mildly retarded children have a distinct growth potential and may so improve their general functioning under a favorable set of circumstances as to move from one of the traditional classifications to the other. . . . In other words what we see emerging in the field of mental retardation is an infinitely more dynamic concept and a more forward-looking optimistic approach. For many of the retardates the progress will be both slow and limited and still keep them largely dependent on the help of others, but that there is movement at all is significant."*

The full impact of Dr. Dybwad's forward thinking and even of his stubborn *fighting* in behalf of the mentally retarded will probably not be felt until several generations have passed. He was always ahead of us, both parents and professional people working for the mentally retarded. Sometimes he was so far ahead that we good-naturedly accused him of being an impractical dreamer, but today we are gradually begin-

* Dybwad, *Challenges in Mental Retardation* (New York: Columbia University Press, 1964), p. 155.

ning to reap the rewards of his farsighted vision, and there is little doubt that the years to come will tend to see some of his "way out" philosophy concerning the mentally retarded fully accepted by parents, by people in the field, and indeed even by the general public at large. It was my personal good fortune as chairman of the Committee on Residential Care for NARC (1959-62) to work closely with Dr. Dybwad and other members of our committee on a detailed study of the state-supported residential centers for the retarded throughout the United States. Among the many other conclusions reached in this *Survey and Study of State Institutions for the Mentally Retarded in the United States** was the fact that residential care need not necessarily be considered as the last resort or as a permanent placement for the retarded person as had generally been true in past years. Instead, it should be looked upon as only one important part of an entire continuum of services available to the mentally retarded from birth to death. Our study led us to promote the idea that, ideally speaking, the mentally retarded should be in position to move into and out of residential care as is demanded by the momentary needs of the retardate and the family situation. Such a philosophy of in and out residential care dictates a whole new concept in the planning for state-supported residential centers for the retarded. To begin with, residential centers must be located near enough to the children served that family ties can be maintained throughout the years. In our own situation we were most fortunate that

---

*Available through National Association for Retarded Children, 420 Lexington Avenue, New York, New York.

the Training School was located only fifty miles from our home, and through the fourteen years Steve was in residence it was fairly easy for us to keep in close contact with him. Unfortunately this is not true for a substantial percent of the more than 200,000 mental retardates of our country who are now in residential care. Many of them are from 200 to 500 miles from their families, and maintaining close family ties under such circumstances is utterly impossible. Today some of our more progressive states are already moving in the direction of developing plans for regional residential care centers which will be located close enough to the families served to make frequent home visits possible. Experience has shown that maintaining a sound relationship with the family is most important if there is to be a successful return of the retardate to full-time family care in future years. Parents, too, must accept the fact that if they hope for the successful return of a retarded child into the family circle, they must be prepared for the necessary adjustments that need to be made. Having a retarded member living in a family whether as a child or as an adult does require certain adjustments on the part of the entire family, and it is important that the family be prepared for this fact.

Recognizing the need for readjustment on our own part as well as that of Steve, we decided to have him home on a trial basis during the fall of 1965 to see if he could work successfully in our family business of manufacturing apple cider. He worked at routine, repetitive tasks that required little or no decision-making on his part. With the help and understanding of all those with whom he worked, his first full-time job was an eminent success. And so long as I live I shall never forget the expression on his face as he came running to the house to show me his first paycheck. The canceled check has gone into the family archives of priceless mementos along with all the other trivia that mothers are accused of accumulating to clutter up the house! I've always maintained, however, that it is just such priceless trivia that turns a mere house into a home, so I just hold on to the children's records of growth and living, clutter or no.

Much of the time during this trial period Steve worked side by side with the faithful Birdie whom he had loved as a little boy. She had recently had surgery, and it was impossible for her to do any heavy lifting, so Steve did the lifting for her. Birdie furnished the brain while Steve furnished the brawn, and between the two of them they made a good team. Another of our employees who had known Steve since infancy taught him how to do some magic tricks with string. He learned to make several difficult designs with his string including Jacob's Ladder, the Turkey Track, and some other patterns having equally romantic names. He spent hours in perfecting his string tricks as well as working out some rather intricate puzzles that had been lying around the house. I had to smile when I remembered all I had heard through the years about the typically short attention span of the mentally retarded. True, their attention span is short, very short, for the things in which they are not interested. But as all parents of retarded children finally learn, their attention span can seem to be forever if it's something in which they are interested instead of in what we want them to be interested.

We found that Mrs. McGuire's string tricks had indeed given Steven a new and joyful dimension in living because for the first time in his life he could now do something better than anyone else, and we were as proud of his accomplishment as if he had discovered the immortal Einstein's theory of relativity. His cup was filled to overflowing when he found that I couldn't do any of these wonderful string tricks and furthermore proved to be a most dull and unapt pupil when he tried in vain to teach me. Our Steve had now discovered one of the greatest joys of young adulthood—the ability to do something better than either of his parents. And no parents in all the whole wide world were so happy to be "outdone" by the accomplishments of a son.

Although Steve will soon return to make his home with us permanently, we will always maintain the appropriate legal status for his return to residential care if and when this might become necessary in future years. We recognize that severe illness within the family, a radical change in Steve's own condition, the death of one or both parents, the normal problems accompanying the aging of parents who may not be able to take care of themselves one day, let alone care for a middle-aged retarded adult—any one or combination of these factors or others may at some time make it necessary that Steve return to the protective environment of residential care. We now know that even though he is capable of partial self-support he will never be able to make his own decisions or manage his own affairs in life with complete independence. But if the time ever becomes necessary for his return, we feel secure in the fact that the readjustment will not be too difficult because he will be returning to familiar scenes, to familiar friends, and to a familiar way of life. He will go, too, secure in the knowledge that on the outside there remain those to whom he belongs and to whom he can return from time to time for the love and affection which is as necessary to the spirit of the mentally retarded as is air to their physical being.

Chapter Eighteen

WHILE STEVIE was making gradual progress within the Lynchburg Training School and Hospital, dramatic progress was being made outside in his behalf as well as for the six million other retardates of our nation. In 1952, when he entered the Training School, there were no public school classes for the trainable retarded child in the state of Virginia. Today over five hundred classes for trainable and educable retarded children are now operating within our public school system, and new ones are being added yearly. In 1947,

when we first began to be concerned about his lack of development, there was not one diagnostic clinic for the retarded within our state and very, very few in the entire nation.
Today there are five such clinics in Virginia alone, with
several hundred in operation throughout the nation. In the
early days of our emotional adjustment to this problem within our family there was no literature available to parents to
explain their problem or give any insight whatever into how
to train or help a mentally retarded child. Today there is a
constantly growing stream of public information available
concerning the retarded. Some of it is prepared specifically
for the parents themselves, although most of it is prepared
with the general public in mind. Books, magazine articles,
movies, TV and radio interviews, newspaper stories—all
are bringing to the public a new and enlightened view of
the rightful place of the mentally retarded in our society.

In spite of the substantial increase in facilities and programs, however, there is still a great need for expansion in
all types of services throughout the entire nation. And even
though the quantity of services is gradually expanding, a
real need exists to develop greater quality in those now being
provided. One of the greatest deterrents to giving the quality
of service needed for the retarded is the serious shortage of
trained personnel. In some cases programs have been established too quickly without having sufficient personnel
to operate them. When the end result is disappointing, the
failure is too often placed on the incapacity of the mentally
retarded themselves rather than on the fact they have been
placed into a situation which has not been conducive to the

proper development of their limited faculties. The NARC has a long-range manpower development program now under way for securing and training individuals to work with the retarded. It is expected that the additional personnel made available through this effort will bring about a gradual improvement within the next decade in both quantity and quality of services provided for the retarded. Today there is much more acceptance of community responsibility in providing for the needs of the retarded, but more is yet needed. Additional special education classes are needed in the public schools; there is a compelling need for day-care centers and activity centers to provide for those retardates who for one reason or another cannot fit into the school programs. This type of care on a community level would, in many cases, sufficiently relieve the stress and strain on the family to the extent that a child might possibly be kept within the family rather than placed in residential care. It would also keep the local community aware of its responsibility to its more helpless citizens. There is also a need for sheltered workshops for the retarded as well as for guidance and direction concerning personal problems for those who may be sufficiently well trained to move into competitive employment. There is need for expansion of programs in recreation, religious nurture, public health nursing services, research and prevention of mental retardation. Research is now going on in many of the major medical centers throughout the country—and indeed throughout the entire world—yet it is recognized by all who are familiar with the intricate details of research that it will take many years and millions of dollars before the ultimate goal is achieved, that of prevention. Speaking before the 1966 annual convention of the Southeastern Region of NARC, President Thomas A. Tucker made this statement: "Ways must be found—indeed will be found—to prevent mental retardation. This is our ultimate goal. It may not be achieved in our lifetime, but what we do now—the research facilities we help to establish, the preventive measures we support—will hasten the day. And until that day arrives the NARC is committed to the task of obtaining for all the mentally retarded the programs and services they require for maximum development of their capabilities."

It has been my personal privilege to have had a small part in this total movement to serve the retarded, and for this privilege of service I shall ever be grateful. None of us who are the parents of these children would have deliberately chosen this path of growth or of service, however. We are too human for that. Pearl S. Buck spoke so eloquently for all parents of the retarded when she wrote these lines: "I cannot say that I am glad my child is retarded. That, indeed would be folly! But I can say, with a full heart, that through her handicap she has brought me into a world of quiet happiness because of renewed faith in human beings." When I look back on the past fifteen years and think of the persons whom I would never have learned to know and love, of the service I might never have been able to give had it not been for the coming of Stevie into our lives, then I am reminded more forcefully than ever of the profound and lasting wisdom of the statement that "all things work together for good to them that love. . . ."

There were many times during my years of effort to serve the retarded, however, when sheer physical, mental, and emotional weariness caused me to stop and ask myself if the price I was paying was too high. Like all parents of such children I sought to find some significance in the total pattern of our lives, some reason for Stevie's being that not only would give meaning to his life but would enable us to make some lasting and worthwhile contribution to the current movement to lift the retarded into their rightful heritage of human compassion. The answer to my questing and some of my deeply personal searching came in a moonlit moment on a Christmas Eve in the mid-1950's, a moment so moving that to this day I have been unable to speak of it at all except to two persons—my husband and a friend who had experienced a somewhat similar soul-shaking occurrence.

Stevie was home from the Training School for Christmas vacation. It was past midnight, and I was taking the poet's "one hour of Christmas for my own." Max and all four children were asleep, and the only sound to be heard in the stillness was the quiet singing of some green applewood logs as they burned on the hearth. I sat by the fire reading, stopping now and then just to savor the warm, gentle peace that enfolded our pine-scented home and to dream of past Christmas Eves that had never failed to fill me with wonder and awe.

The book which I had been reading was Fulton Oursler's *The Greatest Story Ever Told,* and I had just finished the moving description of the Annunciation. Oursler wrote feelingly and with great understanding of the doubts which as-

sailed both Mary and Joseph concerning the humanly in-
explicable event which was to take place in their lives. He
wrote of the frequency with which men in those days pleaded
with God to reveal himself to them through some miraculous
event or through the spoken word or some sign, and how
God, in his infinite understanding of man's need for reassurance, would often give the sign or revelation in order to
give those in doubt the necessary faith to move forward in
their efforts to carry out his total plan. I thought of the eternal
signs of God's promises that are still with us: the rainbow,
the star of the East that led the wise men of old to Bethlehem,
the hope and faith indelibly imprinted on the faces of small
trusting children the world over. For a long time I sat and
pondered on these and other manifestations of God's re-
assuring promises to his wandering and wondering people
down through the ages. How thrilling it would be, I thought,
if such direct communication could take place today for the
guidance and reassurance of war-weary mankind seeking to
find the answers to the perplexing problems of this age.

I had been struggling with some problems of my own.
Decisions had to be made which I knew might very well
affect the entire course of my own life as well as that of
members of my family. My whole being literally ached for
answers to some of the questions that were tormenting me.
I suppose there comes a time in the lives of many persons
when their faith in the future and their reason for being
must be bolstered by something more concrete than stubborn, blind belief. Certainly this need is felt by most of us

who have gone through a real Gethsemane in our personal lives, as have all parents of the mentally retarded.

When we had come face to face with the heart-crushing fact that our beautiful, winsome three-year-old Stevie was mentally retarded, we went through the usual gamut of emotions experienced by most parents who face this stark reality. Our first reaction was disbelief—it just couldn't be. Then came a period of grief so poignant and overwhelming that one longed for death with almost equal intensity with which the instinct of self-preservation forced one to cling to life. This was followed by slow but gradual acceptance that this was just a hard, cold fact of life, and we not only had to learn to live with it but to make the most from it we could. Finally we were caught up with an almost obsessive passion to *do* something about the problem so that parents of such children in years to come need not go through the same bleak, hopeless despair we had experienced in trying to find help for our little son.

Out of this overwhelming passion to do something had come the manuscript for the original edition of *This Is Stevie's Story,* written at the suggestion of Mr. Woodhull Hay, the second president of the National Association for Retarded Children. But after almost one year of writing (most of which was done between three and six A.M. just because there was no other time to do it) and nearly two years spent in trying to place it for publication, the manuscript was still lying in my desk, unpublished. The polite rejection letters from the publishers were so nearly alike that I could soon guess the contents before I opened one. The same phrases occurred over and over again: "Well written but this type story too difficult to promote." "Too much financial risk involved in publishing this type of material." "Subject material unacceptable to our trade." And so on *ad infinitum.* Every once in a while I did have a letter which would indicate that had I been a well-known individual they might have used the material, but since I was totally unknown I suppose they thought the shock value wouldn't be worth much!

In the meantime the manuscript had been read by a number of professional people working in the field of mental retardation as well as a number of parents of retarded children, and all of them urged me to keep trying for publication. Several also offered to help underwrite the cost of publication in case the manuscript was not accepted by a commercial publishing firm. Pearl Buck had offered encouragement and agreed to write the foreword if publication could be arranged. The interest and help of this noted woman, who was not only a Pulitzer Prize winner and a well established writer but a great humanitarian as well, was one of the major factors which gave me the courage to keep going in all the efforts I was putting forth to serve the retarded in those difficult days. In addition to the fact that I was deeply discouraged over the lack of interest in my manuscript, we were faced with what appeared to be many insolvable problems in our newly organized Virginia Association for Retarded Children. I had just about come to the discouraged conclusion that it would be the part of wisdom for me to divorce myself completely from any further activity in the organization, forget about the manuscript, and turn my attention to more satisfying fields of endeavor.

Consequently, here I sat on Christmas Eve after several years of intensive effort in behalf of the retarded with not only an unpublished manuscript but a host of unanswered questions as well. Did the manuscript really have sufficient worth to merit publication? Would it be of value to parents of the retarded, the objective for which both Mr. Hay and I had so hoped? Would the good it might possibly accomplish be worth the mental anguish of baring one's innermost feelings to a public which could quite conceivably misinterpret our motives in taking such a frank and open approach—to a subject which had long been totally taboo for public recognition or discussion? The most disrupting of all the questions which haunted me concerned the amount of time I was now giving to work in behalf of the mentally retarded. I had become so involved in working for their benefit at a local, state, and national level that I was really beginning to have a deep concern that it was too much for my own physical and emotional welfare as well as that of our entire family. And yet there was so much that needed doing that I literally found it impossible to say no when each new opportunity for service presented itself. The many other interests which had made life rich and meaningful for me, such as music, art, family and friends, working with young people in church and camp, had been pushed into the background for the past five years. I had the feeling that my friends and neighbors were beginning to regard me as a lopsided-Lulu-with-a-cause, and the thought frightened me.

As these questions and thoughts passed through my mind on this Christmas Eve, I once more became aware of the opened book in my lap and once again thought of the unparalleled faith of the Virgin Mary as she serenely approached her hour of deliverance, secure in the knowledge that both her own fate and that of the child she would deliver were in God's hands, and no matter what the future might hold she was willing to accept the doing of his will as the dominant factor of her life. But what was his will for my own life? How was I to know that my efforts in behalf of the mentally retarded should continue if it meant the sacrificing of many other interests for my family as well as for myself? Must I keep working to get the manuscript into print, or was this only a waste of time. If only I could be *sure*. If only some sign could be given as had been the case with so many in the days of Mary and Joseph!

Quite suddenly, without the slightest indication of anything supernatural happening, the thought entered my mind that if I would go and simply look at Stevie, somehow I would know what I must do. And fast on the heels of this thought came another—that if I should find his face lying in a pool of moonlight, this would be the "sign" I so hopelessly sought and all doubt would be removed from me forever as to the purpose of my own being or that of Stevie's reason for existence. When the thought first entered my mind, it seemed so preposterous as to be almost laughable. What could I be thinking of? Such things just didn't happen in this day and age. In fact, I was not even certain that the moon was shining on this particular night. Reflecting that

perhaps the magic of Christmas Eve and my own brooding
had brought me near to the point of hallucinating, I picked
up my book and tried once more to read, but every attempt
to center my thinking on anything else always brought me
back to the urgent conclusion that I must go and look at the
sleeping child. Suppose I should go and there was no sign?
Would this, then, be an indication that I should stop trying
to get the manuscript published, cease the multiplicity of my
efforts to help improve the lot of Stevie and the millions like
him? I heard no voice, neither did I see any figure, nor can I
truthfully say that I felt any presence. There was only the
compelling urge, growing more emphatic by the minute, to
get up from my chair and move to the room where Stevie
lay sleeping. For almost an hour I sat staring into the dying
embers of the fire. I was afraid to take the twenty steps to
Stevie's bedside; but I was more afraid not to. Finally indecision became more unbearable than the thought of what
I might or might not find. Trembling with an emotion I
could neither explain or dispel, I went to Stevie's room and
opened the door. There were three windows in the room, all
three in the same wall facing northeast. The room was in
complete darkness save for one small pool of moonlight no
more than fifteen inches square, and that spot of light lay
full and clear on our little retarded son's beautiful, innocent
face. Had I gone to him an hour earlier, the position of the
spot of light in the room would most certainly have been
different because of the passage of the moon across the star-
studded sky; had I gone only seconds later than I did, the
picture would have been different, because even as I knelt

weeping by his bedside the little boy turned on his side and his face was no longer in the full light of the moon but in the dark shadows of the holy night.

I have no explanation for what took place on that Christmas Eve, scientific, psychological, or otherwise. I only know that it happened, and that at this split-second moment I had found the answer to the reason for my own being as well as that of our small son: that the two of us together were destined to use whatever gifts we might possess for the glory of God and for the good of his millions of mentally retarded children, so long as we both should live.

State Associations for Retarded Children

Alabama Association for Retarded Children, P.O. Box 6202, Montgomery, Alabama   36105

Arizona Association for Retarded Children, Inc., 2929 East Thomas Road, Phoenix, Arizona   85016

Arkansas Association for Retarded Children, Inc., University Shopping Center, Mall, Asher at University, Little Rock, Arkansas 72204

California Council for Retarded Children, 1107-9 Street, Sacramento, California   95814

Colorado Association for Retarded Children, Inc., 800 East Colfax Avenue, Denver, Colorado   80218

Connecticut Association for Retarded Children, Inc., 21-R High Street, Hartford, Connecticut   06103

Delaware Association for Retarded Children, Inc., P.O. Box 1896, Wilmington, Delaware   19899

District of Columbia, Help for Retarded Children, Inc., 405 Riggs Road, N.E., Washington, D.C.   20011

Florida Association for Retarded Children, Inc., 313 North Monroe, Tallahassee, Florida   32301

Georgia Association for Retarded Children, Inc., 87 Walton Street, NW, Atlanta, Georgia   30303

Hawaii State Association for Retarded Children, 1018 Lunalilo Street, Honolulu, Hawaii   57457

Idaho Association for Retarded Children, 3221 Crane Creek Road, Boise, Idaho   83702

Illinois Council for Mentally Retarded Children, Inc., 343 South Dearborn Street, Chicago, Illinois   60604

Indiana Association for Retarded Children, Inc., 752 East Market Street, Indianapolis, Indiana   46202

Iowa Association for Retarded Children, Inc., 247 Jewett Building, 9th & Grand Avenue, Des Moines, Iowa   50309

Kansas Association for Retarded Children, Inc., 5830 Nall Avenue, Mission, Kansas 66202

Kentucky Association for Retarded Children, Inc., 315 West Main Street, Frankfort, Kentucky   40601

Louisiana Association for Retarded Children, Old State Capital Building, Baton Rouge, Louisiana   70801

Maine Association for Retarded Children, Inc., P.O. Box 993, Portland, Maine   04104

Maryland Association for Retarded Children, Inc., 1514 Reisterstown Road, Pikesville, Maryland   21208

Massachusetts Association for Retarded Children, Inc., 409 Lexington Street, Auburndale, Massachusetts   02166

Michigan Association for Retarded Children, 510 Michigan National Tower, Lansing, Michigan   48933

Minnesota Association for Retarded Children, Inc., 6315 Penn Avenue South, Minneapolis, Minnesota   55423

Mississippi Association for Retarded Children, Inc., 145 East Amite Street, Jackson, Mississippi 39201

Missouri Association for Retarded Children, 100 West Dunklin, Jefferson City, Missouri   65101

Montana Association for Retarded Children, 640 North Rodney, Helena, Montana   59601

Nebraska Association for Retarded Children, 1711 South 22, Lincoln, Nebraska   68502

Nevada Association for Retarded Children, 3000 Vegas Drive, Las Vegas, Nevada   89106

New Hampshire Council for Retarded Children, 521 Maple Street, Manchester, New Hampshire   03104

New Jersey Association for Retarded Children, Inc., 97 Bayard Street, New Brunswick, New Jersey   08901

New Mexico Association for Retarded Children, 9401 LaGrima de oro Road, N.E., Albuquerque, New Mexico   87111

New York State Association for Retarded Children, Inc., 19 Union Square, New York, New York   10003

North Carolina Association for Retarded Children, Inc., P.O. Box 11042, Charlotte, North Carolina   28209

North Dakota Association for Retarded Children, Inc., Box 1494, Fargo, North Dakota   58103

Ohio Association for Retarded Children, Inc., 131 East State Street, Columbus, Ohio   43215

Oklahoma Association for Mentally Retarded Children, Inc., 30 North Hudson, Oklahoma City, Oklahoma   73102

Oregon Association for Retarded Children, P.O. Box 7186, Salem, Oregon   97303

Pennsylvania Association for Retarded Children, Inc., 112 North Second Street, Harrisburg, Pennsylvania   17101

Rhode Island Association for Retarded Children, Inc., 385 Westminster Street, Providence, Rhode Island   02903

South Carolina Association for Retarded Children, Inc., P.O. Box 1564, Columbia, South Carolina   29202

South Dakota Association for Retarded Children, Inc., 1612 West 41 Street, Sioux Falls, South Dakota   57105

Tennessee Association for Retarded Children and Adults, Inc., 1701-21st Avenue, South, Nashville, Tennessee   37212

Texas Association for Retarded Children, Inc., 706 Littlefield Building, 6th & Congress, Austin, Texas   78701

Utah Association for Retarded Children, P.O. Box 686, Salt Lake City, Utah   84110

Vermont Association for Retarded Children, Inc., P.O. Box 457, Bennington, Vermont   05201

Virginia Association for Retarded Children, Inc., 10 South 10 Street, Richmond, Virginia   23219

Washington Association for Retarded Children, 205 East 14 Avenue, Olympia, Washington   98502

West Virginia Association for Retarded Children, Inc., 420 Wilson Court, Huntington, West Virginia   25701

Wisconsin Association for Retarded Children, Inc., 119 East Washington Avenue, Madison, Wisconsin   53703

Wyoming Association for Retarded Children, P.O. Box 790, Thermopolis, Wyoming   82443